PERSPECTIVES 11

DIVIDED IRELAND

edited by Noreen O'Donovan

Ernst Klett Schulbuchverlag
Stuttgart Düsseldorf Berlin Leipzig

Herausgegeben von Noreen O'Donovan, Pforzheim.
Beratende Mitarbeit: Professor Hans-Joachim Lechler,
Fachleiter für Englisch am Seminar für Studienreferendare, Esslingen.

Abbreviations and symbols used in this book:

arch.	archaic	etc.	et cetera	opp.	opposite
bib.	biblical	Gael.	Gaelic	p./pp.	page(s)
Co.	County	i. e.	that is	pl.	plural
cf.	compare	Ir.	Irish	rel.	religious
coll.	colloquial	l./ll.	line(s)	sg.	singular
dial.	dialect	lit.	literary	sl.	slang
derog.	derogatory	n.	noun	s. o.	someone
e. g.	for example	N.I.	Northern Ireland	s. th.	something
esp.	especially	o. s.	oneself	v.	against

→G see Glossary, page 62
→H see Chronology of Irish History, page 6

Texts marked with this sign are included on the cassette which accompanies this book (Klettnummer 513712).

In the vocabulary notes, words printed in **bold** are particularly important; it would be a good idea to learn them. Words printed in *italics* will help you to understand the text you are reading, but need not be memorized.

Picture Credits:

Jack Clafferty (drawing for Information on Ireland, London): p. 60; Cummings cartoon © 1982: p. 61; Mary Evans Picture Library, London: pp. 19, 56; Hulton Picture Library, London: pp. 22, 25, 52; Industrial Development Authority, Dublin: p. 46; Keystone Pressedienst, Hamburg: pp. 5 t.r./m.r., 16, 19; The Mansell Collection, London: p. 12 t./b.; Mercier Press, Cork: map p. 23; Noreen O'Donovan, Pforzheim: p. 5 m.l./b.l./b.r.; Pacemaker Press, Belfast: pp. 36, 42, 55; Popperfoto, London: p. 5 t.l., 17; Derek Speirs/ Report, Dublin: pp. 34, 53, cover.

The cover photograph shows some participants in a loyalist parade in Belfast. To the traditional flag of Ulster has been added a crown and a Union Jack, symbolizing union with Britain. (Derek Speirs/Report)

1. Auflage 1 5 4 3 | 1994 93 92

Alle Drucke dieser Auflage können im Unterricht nebeneinander benutzt werden, sie sind untereinander unverändert. Die letzte Zahl bezeichnet das Jahr dieses Druckes.

Fotosatz: SCS Schwarz Satz & Bild digital, L.-Echterdingen
Druck: Stuttgarter Druckerei, Stuttgart. Printed in Germany

ISBN 3-12-513710-1

Contents

By Way of Introduction: The Island

They say the skies of Lebanon are burning
Those mighty cedars bleeding in the heat
They're showing pictures on the television
Women and children dying in the street
And we're still at it in our own place
Still trying to reach the future through the past
Still trying to carve tomorrow from a tombstone…

Chorus: But hey! Don't listen to me
Cos this wasn't meant to be no sad song
We've heard too much of that before
Right now I only want to be here with you
Till the morning dew comes falling
I want to take you to the island
And trace your footprints in the sand
And in the evening when the sun goes down
We'll make love to the sound of the ocean

They're raising banners over by the markets
Whitewashing slogans on the shipyard walls
Witchdoctors praying for a mighty showdown
No way our holy flag is gonna fall
Up here we sacrifice our children
To feed the worn-out dreams of yesterday
And teach them dying will lead us into glory… *(Repeat chorus)*

Now I know us plain folks don't see all the story
And I know this peace and love's just copping out
And I guess these young boys dying in the ditches
Is just what being free is all about
And how this twisted wreckage down on Main Street
Will bring us all together in the end
And we'll go marching down the road to freedom…
Freedom

Music and lyrics by Paul Brady.

2 *cedar* ['si:də] an evergreen tree for which Lebanon was famous even in biblical times – 7 **tombstone** ['tu:mstəʊn] slab of stone marking a grave – 12 **dew** moisture that falls from the air when it cools – 14 **to trace** to follow the path or outline of s. th. – 17 **banner** flag held with two poles and displaying a political (or other) slogan, symbol, etc. – 18 *to whitewash* here: to write with the white paint usually used for painting walls – **slogan** ['sləʊgən] simple, striking expression of a political (or other) belief, demand, etc. – **shipyard** place where ships are built (a reference to Belfast's shipbuilding industry) – 19 *witchdoctor* tribal "medicine man"; here derog.: political leader – *showdown* final conflict (as between hero and villain in a Western movie) – 20 *No way…* (coll.) … cannot be allowed to happen – *gonna* (sl.) going to – 21 **to sacrifice** ['sækrɪfaɪs] to give up, or to allow to die (as part of a religious ritual) – 24 *us plain folks* (sl.) we ordinary people – 25 *to cop out* (coll.) to give up, to avoid dealing with a difficult issue – 26 **ditch** drainage channel along a hedge surrounding a field – 28 **wreckage** the remains of s. th. that has been destroyed

1. *Try to explain the images in lines 6–7.*
2. *In the chorus, the speaker expresses a very common reaction to the present "troubles" in Northern Ireland. What is it?*
3. *What role is attributed to the political leaders?*
4. *What political arguments are acknowledged in the final verse? How do you know what the speaker's real feelings are?*
5. *How important do you think it is to know "all the story" (l. 24)?*

A Chronology of Irish History

c. 200 B.C. Celtic speaking peoples arrive in Ireland.

432 St Patrick comes to Ireland to spread Christianity, which leads to a "Golden Age" of religion, art and scholarship.

795 The Vikings begin to raid the Irish monasteries and form settlements of their own, until defeated in 1014.

1169 The Anglo-Normans invade Ireland and gain control of most of the country; many Gaelic chieftains remain powerful (origin of English-Irish conflict).

1536 Henry VIII's attempt to impose Reformation on the Irish remains unsuccessful (origin of religious conflict).

1601 The rebel Ulster chieftains O'Neill and O'Donnell are defeated by the forces of Elizabeth I at Kinsale, where they had hoped to join up with their Spanish allies.

1607 The departure of the Irish chieftains into exile is soon followed by the "Plantation" of Ulster with Protestant settlers from Britain (origin of Ulster conflict).

1641 A Catholic rebellion breaks out in Ulster.

1649 After the English Civil War, Oliver Cromwell carries out a campaign of revenge on the Irish Catholic population; thousands are slaughtered; land ownership is transferred to Protestants all over the country (creation of a Protestant upper class).

1691 The Jacobite Wars (named after James II of England) end in defeat of his Catholic supporters by William III (William of Orange); the Battle of the Boyne, 1690, becomes a symbol of Protestant supremacy; "Penal Laws" oppressing Catholics come in force.

1798 After the failure of parliamentary reforms, Wolfe Tone's "United Irishmen" rebel in Ulster and Wexford; French aid arrives too late to prevent defeat.

1800 British power is consolidated by abolishing the Irish Parliament (Act of Union).

1829 A mass movement led by Daniel O'Connell achieves Catholic Emancipation; his movement for the repeal of the Act of Union is less successful.

1846 The Great Famine: Failure of the potato crop causes starvation, death and mass emigration among the miserably poor Irish peasants; at the same time, grain is exported by landlords as a cash crop.

1848 The "Young Ireland" movement is formed; their rebellion fails.

1858 The Irish Republican Brotherhood (or Fenian Movement) is founded.

1867 A Fenian rising is suppressed in various parts of the country.

1877 Charles Stuart Parnell begins the parliamentary movement for Home Rule.

1879 The National Land League is founded; their campaigns lead to reforms in the landlord system and eventual restoration of land ownership to the peasants (1903).

1886 Gladstone's first Home Rule bill is rejected.

1893 Gladstone's second Home Rule bill is rejected in the House of Lords.
The Gaelic League is founded – a movement to restore Irish language and culture.

1912 The Ulster Volunteers are formed by Sir Edward Carson to resist the Home Rule planned for Ireland (third Home Rule Bill).

1913 A general strike in Dublin is followed by lock-outs and social unrest; the Citizen Army is founded to protect the workers.
The Irish Volunteers are formed in response to Carson.

1914 The Home Rule Bill receives royal assent, but its operation is suspended because of the outbreak of World War I.

1916 The Easter Rising in Dublin is defeated; the execution of the leaders shocks the Irish public.

1918 The radical republican party Sinn Féin wins a landslide victory in the general election; instead of taking their seats in Westminster they set up an alternative republican parliament and legislative system.

1919 The Anglo-Irish War, or War of Independence begins; Britain sends the notorious "Black and Tans" auxiliary force to fight what is now the IRA.

1921 The war ends with a Treaty creating two Irish states:
- 6 Ulster Counties to remain within the United Kingdom;
- the 26-county Free State to be outside the UK but within the Commonwealth.

Northern Ireland		**Republic of Ireland**	
1922	An armed police force (RUC) and special constabularies are set up to suppress violent anti-partition protest; the Special Powers Act gives them very wide powers to arrest and detain suspects.	1922	Civil War between pro- and anti-Treaty forces; the latter capitulate in 1923.
1935	Many people are killed in an outbreak of sectarian violence in Belfast.	1937	The Free State declared a Republic (recognized by Britain in 1949); Constitution contains Catholic elements.
1939	Outbreak of World War II; Belfast suffers bombing.	1939	The Republic stays neutral in World War II.

1956 The IRA begins a series of attacks on the Northern Ireland border; the campaign is abandoned five years later for lack of public support.

1964 A "Campaign for Social Justice" is begun by two private citizens; they want an end to discrimination against Catholics.

1965 The first meeting ever between the Prime Ministers of N. Ireland and the Republic.

1967 The N. I. Civil Rights Association is formed.

1968 Thousands take part in Civil Rights marches, some of which end in clashes with police and counter-demonstrators; in November the Government announces a reform programme.

1969 A students' march from Belfast to Derry is violently attacked by Protestants; the RUC is accused of sympathizing with the attackers; months of rioting and sectarian violence follow.
In August, the British Army is brought in to restore order.

	Northern Ireland		Republic of Ireland
1970	Army tactics (searches, curfews) lose them the sympathy of the Catholics; the IRA becomes established as their "protectors" in working-class areas.		
1971	An IRA bombing campaign claims many lives; a new organization, the Protestant UDA, adopts similar methods. Internment without trial is introduced (ended 1975).		
1972	"Bloody Sunday": On 30 January 13 young men are shot by British paratroopers after a demonstration. In March the Stormont Government is suspended; direct rule from Westminster is imposed.	1972	By referendum, the special position of the Catholic Church is removed from the Constitution.
1973	Both the United Kingdom (including Northern Ireland) and the Republic of Ireland join the European Economic Community. Elections under proportional representation are held for a new N. I. Assembly.		
1974	After the Sunningdale Agreement a new "power-sharing" executive is set up which is acceptable to Catholics; a few months later (May) it is brought down by a loyalist general strike, and direct rule is re-imposed.		
1976	IRA prisoners lose political status; the "H-Block Campaign" protests begin.		
1977	The "Peace People" demand an end to the violence and gain much support; the leaders Mairead Corrigan and Betty Williams are awarded the Nobel Peace Prize, but their influence declines after a few years.		
1981	Ten IRA prisoners die on hunger strike for recognition as political prisoners.		
1982	New Assembly with restricted powers is elected, but is boycotted by the minority (dissolved again 1986).	1982	By referendum, an amendment banning abortion is added to the Constitution.
1985	The Anglo-Irish Agreement gives the Republic a consultative role in Northern Ireland through an inter-governmental Conference; loyalist protests fail to stop it.		
1986	The Stalker inquiry into allegations of an RUC "shoot-to-kill" policy runs into difficulties, and John Stalker is removed on a pretext.	1986	The proposal to remove the ban on divorce from the Constitution is rejected.
1987	IRA atrocity in Enniskillen shocks the public.		
1988	Three unarmed IRA members are killed in Gibraltar by the SAS; the inquest concludes that the killings were "lawful", but considerable doubt remains.		
1989	IRA attacks on British Army in West Germany.		

I Britain's First Colony

1 The State of Ireland

At the beginning of the year 1845 the state of Ireland was, as it had been for nearly seven hundred years, a source of grave anxiety to England. Ireland had first been invaded in 1169; it was now 1845, yet she had been neither assimilated nor subdued. The country had been conquered not once but several times, the land had been confiscated and redistributed over and over again, the population had been brought to the verge of extinction – after Cromwell's conquest and settlement only some half million Irish survived – yet an Irish nation still existed, separate, numerous and hostile. [...]

The hostility between England and Ireland, which six centuries had failed to extinguish, had its roots first of all in race. After the first invasions, the first conquests, the Irish hated the English with the hatred of the defeated and the dispossessed. Nevertheless, eventually the English and the Irish might have fused, as the English and the Scots, the English and the Welsh have, for practical purposes, fused, had it not been that in the sixteenth century racial animosity was disastrously strengthened by religious enmity.

The crucial event was the Reformation. The ideas of liberty which the English cherish and the history of their country's rise to greatness are bound up with Protestantism, while Ireland, alone among the countries of northern Europe, was scarcely touched by the Reformation. The gulf which resulted could never be bridged. In the political division of Europe which followed the Reformation, England and Ireland were on opposing sides. Henceforward, Irish aspirations could only be fulfilled, Irish faith could only flourish, through the defeat of England and the triumph of her enemies.

Freedom for Ireland meant Philip of Spain and the Inquisition in place of Elizabeth I, it meant James II instead of William III, it even meant, since misery and oppression make strange bedfellows, the victory of Napoleon.

So completely is the history of the one country the reverse of the history of the other that the very names which to an Englishman mean glory, victory and prosperity to an Irishman spell degradation, misery and ruin. In Ireland the name of Elizabeth I stands only for the horrors of her Irish conquest; in the defeat of the Armada, Ireland's hopes of independence went down; above all, with the name of William III and the glorious revolution of 1688, the very foundation of British liberties, the Catholic Irishman associates only the final subjugation of his country and the degradation and injustice of the Penal Laws. Freedom for the one meant slavery for the other; victory for the one meant defeat for the other; the good of the one was the evil of the other. Ireland, resentful and hostile, lying only a day's sail, in fine weather, from Britain's coasts, for centuries provided a refuge for enemy agents, a hatching-ground for enemy plots; her motto was "England's difficulty is Ireland's opportunity," and in every crisis of England's history she seized the moment of weakness to stab her enemy in the back. It is the explanation, if not the excuse, for the ferocity with which the English have treated Ireland.

In the eighteen-forties, after nearly seven hundred years of English domination, Irish poverty and Irish misery appalled the traveller. [...] All this wretchedness and misery could, almost without exception, be traced to a single source – the system under which land had come to be occupied and owned in Ireland, a system produced by centuries of successive conquests, rebellions, confiscations and punitive legislation.

From *The Great Hunger* by Cecil Woodham-Smith, London: Hamish Hamilton Ltd. 1962, pp. 9, 12–15.

6 **to assimilate** to take in and make part of a greater whole – **to subdue** to conquer, to control or make calm – 8 **to confiscate** ['–––] to take away from the owner by authority of the state – 9 **to redistribute** [––'––] to divide anew and give to different people – 10 **to the verge of** near – **extinction** dying out – 11 *(Oliver) Cromwell* English Puritan Dictator from 1649–58 (→**H**) – 14 **hostile** unfriendly, as of an enemy – 16 **to extinguish** to put out (a fire), to end – 20 **dispossessed** deprived of one's possessions, esp. land – 21 *to fuse* to blend together and form a larger unit – 25 **animosity, enmity** hostility, hatred – 27 **crucial** ['kru:ʃəl] decisive, most important – 28 **to cherish** ['tʃerɪʃ] to hold dear, to value highly – 30 **bound up with** closely connected with – 33 *to bridge a gulf* to cross a large gap – 36 *henceforward* from then on – 37 *aspiration* hope – 38 **faith** here: religion – 42 *Elizabeth I* (Protestant) Queen of England from 1558–1603 – 43 *Philip* (Catholic) King of Spain, enemy of Elizabeth I – *James II* (Catholic) King of England who was replaced in 1688 by the Protestant William III – 44 **misery** great suffering – **oppression** the harsh suppression of a people – 45 *bedfellows* (fig.) companions – *Napoleon (Bonaparte)* French Emperor who was at war with Britain 1803–05 – 49 **prosperity** economic well-being, wealth – 50 **degradation** humiliation – 53 *Armada* the Spanish fleet that tried in vain to invade England (1588) – 55 *glorious revolution* to prevent a Catholic coming to the throne, Parliament gave the crown to Queen Mary, Protestant daughter of James II and her husband, William of Orange, or William III (also →**H**, 1691) – 58 *subjugation* total conquest – 59 *Penal Laws* laws excluding Catholics from public life and ownership of property, and suppressing practice of their religion (→**H**) – 65 *refuge* ['––] safe place – 66 *hatching ground* place where s. th. can develop (as an egg is hatched in a bird's nest) – 69 **to stab** to cut with the point of a dagger or knife – 71 *ferocity* fierceness, cruelty – 75 **to appall** to shock – 76 *wretchedness* misery, suffering – 77 *to trace to* to find the explanation for s. th. in – 80 *successive* one after another – 81 **punitive** ['pju:n––] as punishment

1. *What was the situation in Ireland in the early 19th century?*
2. *Scotland also suffered from English colonization. Why, according to the author, were the results so different?*
3. *List the English heroes mentioned here. What do you know about them?*
4. *What enemies of England are mentioned? Why were they enemies? Why should the native Irish support them?*

2 Rebels and Loyalists: A Short History in Song

a) Follow Me Up to Carlow

Fiach MacHugh O'Byrne was one of the many Gaelic chieftains who resisted the spread of English power in Ireland. At the time, the forces of Queen Elizabeth I had full control only of "the Pale", a strip of land along the east coast around the city of Dublin.

The words of the following song refer to Fiach McHugh's success in uniting a number of other chieftains and feudal lords to defeat the Queen's Lord Deputy, Lord Grey de Wilton, at the Pass of Glenmalure (just outside the Pale) in 1580.

Lift, MacCahir Og, your face,
Brooding o'er the old disgrace
That black Fitzwilliam stormed your place
And drove you to the fern!
Grey said victory was sure,
Soon the firebrand he'd secure,
Until he met at Glenmalure
With Fiach MacHugh O'Byrne!

Chorus: Curse and swear, Lord Kildare!
Fiach will do what Fiach will dare!
Now Fitzwilliam, have a care,
Fallen is your star low!
Up with halberd, out with sword!
On we'll go, for by the Lord,
Fiach MacHugh has given the word:
"Follow me up to Carlow."

See the swords of Glen Imale
Flashing o'er the English Pale!
See all the children of the Gael
Beneath O'Byrne's banners!
Rooster of a fighting stock,
Would you let a Saxon cock
Crow out upon an Irish rock?
Fly up and teach him manners! (*Chorus*)

From Tassagart to Clonmore
There flows a stream of Saxon gore,
Och, great is Rory Og O'More
At sending loons to Hades!
White is sick, Lane is fled,
Now for black Fitzwilliam's head,
We'll send it over dripping red
To Queen Liza and her ladies! (*Chorus*)

Words by Patrick Joseph McCall to a traditional tune.

1 *MacCahir Og* [məˈkeər ˈoːg] (Gael., = Young MacCahir) a minor chieftain, or clan leader – 2 **to brood (over s. th.)** to think constantly about s. th. bad or sad – *o'er* (lit.) over – **disgrace** s. th. that causes loss of respect – 3 *black* here: a derogatory term – *Fitzwilliam* nobleman in the service of the Queen, later Lord Deputy – 4 *to the fern* here: away, into the country – 5 *Grey* see introduction – 6 **firebrand** person who causes unrest; rebel – *to secure* here: to capture – 7 *Glenmalure* [ˌ––ˈ–] valley and mountain pass in County Wicklow (see introduction) – 9 **to curse** to swear, to wish misfortune on s. o. – *Lord Kildare* feudal lord loyal (at this time) to the Queen – 13 *halberd* weapon that cuts like an axe – 16 *Carlow* town and county south-west of Dublin – 17 *Glen Imale* valley in Co. Wicklow – 18 *Pale* (see introduction) – 19 *the Gael* the native (Gaelic) Irish – 20 **banner** flag – 21 **rooster** cock – *stock* family, ancestry, kind – 22 **Saxon** here: English (as opposed to the Celtic Irish) – 23 **to crow** to make the sound of a cock – 25 *Tassagart, Clonmore* places in Counties Wicklow and Carlow – 26 **gore** blood that is shed – 27 *Rory Og O'More* another Gaelic chieftain – 28 *loon* (coll.) fool, worthless or insane person – *Hades* [ˈheɪdiːz] hell – 29 *White* English colonist – *Lane* Ralph Lane, English colonist who went on to help establish the colonies in North America – 32 *Liza* here: Queen Elizabeth I

1. *What people are spoken to in this song? And what sentiments are expressed in each case?*
2. *What is supposed to unite the rebels against the Queen?*

b) The Green Grassy Slopes of the Boyne

The Protestant settlers in Ireland had good reason to fear the rebels, who were mainly Catholics. This is why they welcomed the defeat of the Catholic King James by their hero, William of Orange, at the Boyne river in 1690.

Some folk sing of the mountains and valleys,
Where the wild flow'rs abundantly grow,
And some of the foam-crested billows
That dash in the waters below;
But I'm going to sing of a river,
And I hope in the chorus you'll join,
Of the deeds that were done by King William
On the green grassy slopes of the Boyne!

Chorus:
On the green grassy slopes of the Boyne,
Where the Orangemen with William did join,
And they fought for our glorious deliverance
On the green grassy slopes of the Boyne.

On the banks of that beautiful river,
There the bones of our forefathers lie,
Awaiting the sound of the trumpet
To call them to glory on high;
In our hearts we will cherish their mem'ries,
And we all like true brethren will join,
And praise God for sending us King William
To the green grassy slopes of the Boyne.
(*Chorus*)

Orangemen will be loyal and steady,
For no matter what e'er may betide
We will still mind our war-cry "No Surrender"
So long as we've God on our side.
And if ever our service is needed
Then we all like true brethren will join
And fight like our valiant King William
On the green grassy slopes of the Boyne.
(*Chorus*)

The victory of King William on the 12th July 1690 still plays an important part in Protestant mythology. *(See pages 17, 27.)*

2 **abundantly** plentifully – 3 *foam-crested* foam on top – *billow* wave – 4 *to dash* to splash against s. th. – 8 **slope** land that rises or falls – 10 *Orangemen* Protestant supporters of William of Orange; later, members of the Orange Order (→**G**) – 11 *deliverance* salvation – 14 **forefathers** ancestors – 15 *the trumpet*… i. e. of the Last Judgement – 17 **to cherish** [tʃerɪʃ] to hold dear – 18 **brethren** (arch./rel.) brothers, comrades – 22 *what e'er may betide* (arch.) what ever may happen – 23 *to mind* here: to heed, to remember – 27 *valiant* brave, heroic

1. *What, according to the song, did William achieve at the Battle of the Boyne?*
2. *What do you think is meant by line: "… if ever our service is needed" (l. 25)?*

Theobald Wolfe Tone, a Protestant lawyer, was influenced by the French Revolution. He succeeded in uniting Catholics and liberal Protestants to campaign for democracy, and in persuading the French to send military help. Two French fleets did land in 1798, but too late to help the United Irishmen. Tone was captured on board a French ship and sentenced to death.

c) Roddy McCorley

One of the many rebel songs about heroes who died in the cause of Irish freedom. Roddy McCorley had taken part in the ill-fated rebellion of 1798.

See the fleet-foot host of men
Who speed with faces wan
From farmstead and from fisher's cot
Upon the banks of Bann!
They come with vengeance in their eyes,
Too late, too late are they, –
For young Roddy McCorley goes to die
On the Bridge of Toome today!

Up the narrow street he steps,
Smiling, proud and young.
About the hemp rope on his neck
The golden ringlets clung.
There's never a tear in his blue eyes,
Both glad and bright are they
As young Roddy McCorley goes to die
On the Bridge of Toome today.

When he last stepped up that street,
His shining pike in hand,
Behind him marched in grim array
A stalwart earnest band.
For Antrim town! For Antrim town!
He led them to the fray –
And young Roddy McCorley goes to die
On the Bridge of Toome today!

There was never a one of all your dead
More bravely fell in fray
Than he who marches to his fate
On the Bridge of Toome today.
True to the last, true to the last
He treads the upward way,
And young Roddy McCorley goes to die
On the Bridge of Toome today.

Words and music by Ethna Carbery.

1 *fleet-foot* (lit.) quick-moving – **host** [həʊst] great number, army – 2 **wan** [wɒn] pale, looking ill – 3 *cot* (lit.) cottage – 4 *Bann* river in the north of Ireland – 5 *vengeance* revenge – 8 *Toome* village in County Antrim – 11 *hemp-rope* rope of strong fibres, here used for hanging – 18 *pike* long wooden shaft with a spearhead, formerly used by soldiers and rebels – 19 *array* order – 20 *stalwart* tall and muscular – 21 *Antrim* the town from which Co. Antrim took its name – 22 *fray* fight

1. *From the information given in the song, reconstruct as many of the facts as possible.*
2. *What characteristics of the young man are stressed? Why?*
3. *Is it a good thing to be willing to die for one's ideals? What do you think? What does the song suggest?*
4. *Both pictures on the left are by British artists. Discuss the impression they are meant to give.*

II The National Revival

1 Encounter with Miss Ivors

James Joyce's famous story, "The Dead" describes a party held in Dublin at the turn of the century. In the course of the evening the hero, Gabriel Conroy, is forced to reconsider his attitude to many things. The following incident reveals a lot about the political situation in Ireland at the time.

Lancers were arranged. Gabriel found himself partnered with Miss Ivors. She was a frank-mannered, talkative young lady, with a freckled face and prominent brown eyes. She did not wear a low-cut bodice, and the large brooch which was fixed in the front of her collar bore on it an Irish device and motto.

When they had taken their places she said abruptly:

'I have a crow to pluck with you.'

'With me?' said Gabriel.

She nodded her head gravely.

'What is it?' asked Gabriel, smiling at her solemn manner.

'Who is G. C.?' answered Miss Ivors, turning her eyes upon him.

Gabriel coloured and was about to knit his brows, as if he did not understand, when she said bluntly:

'O, innocent Amy! I have found out that you write for *The Daily Express*. Now, aren't you ashamed of yourself?'

'Why should I be ashamed of myself?' asked Gabriel, blinking his eyes and trying to smile.

'Well, I'm ashamed of you,' said Miss Ivors frankly. 'To say you'd write for a paper like that. I didn't think you were a West Briton.'

A look of perplexity appeared on Gabriel's face. It was true that he wrote a literary column every Wednesday in *The Daily Express*, for which he was paid fifteen shillings. But that did not make him a West Briton surely. The books he received for review were almost more welcome than the paltry cheque. He loved to feel the covers and turn over the pages of newly printed books. Nearly every day when his teaching in the college was ended he used to wander down the quays to the second-hand booksellers, to Hickey's on Bachelor's Walk, to Webb's or Massey's on Aston's Quay, or to O'Clohissey's in the by-street. He did not know how to meet her charge. He wanted to say that literature was above politics. But they were friends of many years' standing and their careers had been parallel, first at the University and then as teachers: he could not risk a grandiose phrase with her. He continued blinking his eyes and trying to smile and murmured lamely that he saw nothing political in writing reviews of books.

When their turn to cross had come he was still perplexed and inattentive. Miss Ivors promptly took his hand in a warm grasp and said in a soft friendly tone:

'Of course, I was only joking. Come, we cross now.'

When they were together again she spoke of the University question and Gabriel felt more at ease. A friend of hers had shown her his review of Browning's poems. That was how she had found out the secret: but she liked the review immensely. Then she said suddenly:

'O, Mr Conroy, will you come for an excursion to the Aran Isles this summer? We're going to stay there a whole month. It will be splendid out in the Atlantic. You ought to come. Mr Clancy is coming, and Mr Kilkelly and Kathleen Kearney. It would be splendid for Gretta too if she'd come. She's from Connacht, isn't she?'

'Her people are,' said Gabriel shortly.

'But you will come, won't you?' said Miss Ivors, laying her warm hand eagerly on his arm.

'The fact is,' said Gabriel, 'I have just arranged to go –'

'Go where?' asked Miss Ivors.

'Well, you know, every year I go for a cycling tour with some fellows and so –'

'But where?' asked Miss Ivors.

'Well, we usually go to France or Belgium or perhaps Germany,' said Gabriel awkwardly.

'And why do you go to France and Belgium,' said Miss Ivors, 'instead of visiting your own land?'

'Well,' said Gabriel, 'it's partly to keep in touch with the languages and partly for a change.'

'And haven't you your own language to keep in touch with – Irish?' asked Miss Ivors.

'Well,' said Gabriel, 'if it comes to that, you know, Irish is not my language.'

Their neighbours had turned to listen to the cross-examination. Gabriel glanced right and left nervously and tried to keep his good humour under the ordeal, which was making a blush invade his forehead.

'And haven't you your own land to visit,' continued Miss Ivors, 'that you know nothing of, your own people, and your own country?'

'O, to tell you the truth,' retorted Gabriel suddenly, 'I'm sick of my own country, sick of it!'

'Why?' asked Miss Ivors.

Gabriel did not answer, for his retort had heated him.

'Why?' repeated Miss Ivors.

They had to go visiting together and, as he had not answered her, Miss Ivors said warmly:

'Of course, you've no answer.'

Gabriel tried to cover his agitation by taking part in the dance with great energy. He avoided her eyes, for he had seen a sour expression on her face. But when they met in the long chain he was surprised to feel his hand firmly pressed. She looked at him from under her brows for a moment quizzically until he smiled. Then, just as the chain was about to start again, she stood on tiptoe and whispered into his ear:

'West Briton!'

When the lancers were over Gabriel went away to a remote corner of the room where Freddy Malins' mother was sitting. She was a stout, feeble old woman with white hair. Her voice had a catch in it like her son's and she stuttered slightly. She had been told that Freddy had come and that he was nearly all right. Gabriel asked her whether she had had a good crossing. She lived with her married daughter in Glasgow and came to Dublin on a visit once a year. She answered placidly that she had had a beautiful crossing and that the captain had been most attentive to her. She spoke also of the beautiful house her daughter kept in Glasgow, and of all the friends they had there. While her tongue rambled on Gabriel tried to banish from his mind all memory of the unpleasant incident with Miss Ivors. Of course the girl, or woman, or whatever she was, was an enthusiast, but there was a time for all things. Perhaps he ought not to have answered her like that. But she had no right to call him a West Briton before people, even in joke. She had tried to make him ridiculous before people, heckling him and staring at him with her rabbit's eyes.

From the story "The Dead" in *Dubliners* by James Joyce, London 1914.

5 *lancers* a group dance – 7 **frank** open, honest – 8 **freckled** with brown spots on the skin – 9 *bodice* ['bɒdɪs] top of a dress – 10 **brooch** [əʊ] piece of jewellery pinned to one's clothes – 11 *Irish device* Celtic motif – 14 *a crow to pluck…* s. th. annoying that needs to be talked about – 18 **solemn** ['sɒləm] serious – 21 *to knit one's brows* to frown – 23 **bluntly** very directly – 24 *innocent Amy* (dated sl.) an exclamation of surprise at s. o.'s seeming innocence (here, Gabriel's lack of knowledge of his "crime") – 25 *Daily Express* a conservative newspaper, opposed to the various national movements current at the time – 32 *West Briton* (derog.) an Irish person who identifies with Britain – 33 *perplexity* puzzlement – 36 *fifteen shillings* old currency (equals 75p, not allowing for inflation) – 38 *for review* in order to write a critical article about – 39 **paltry** [ɔː] very small, insignificant – 43 *quays* here: banks of the river Liffey – 49 *of many years' standing* for a long time – 52 *grandiose* high-sounding – 56 *to cross* to change sides in the dance – 57 **inattentive** not paying attention – 63 *the University question* the controversy surrounding Dublin's universities, the older of which (Trinity College) was regarded as exclusively Protestant, leading to the foundation of University Col-

lege (Catholic) – 65 *Browning* Robert Browning (1812–1889), English poet – 70 *Aran Isles* islands off the west coast of Ireland, noted for the preservation of Irish (Gaelic) language and way of life – 75 *Gretta* Gabriel's wife – *Connacht* ['kɒnəxt] western province of Ireland – 79 **eager** enthusiastic – 88 **awkwardly** uncomfortably – 100 **cross-examination** questioning as in a court of law – 102 **ordeal** difficult experience – 103 **blush** a slight reddening of the skin – 111 **retort** angry answer – 114 *go visiting... long chain* elements in the dance – 123 *quizzically* questioningly – 129 **remote** far away – 131 **stout** rather fat – **feeble** weak (with old age) – 134 *nearly all right* here: nearly sober, not too drunk – 136 *crossing* journey across the Irish sea – 138 **placidly** calmly – 144 **to banish** to dismiss, to put out (of his mind) – 147 **enthusiast** person with a very active interest in s. th. – 152 **to heckle** to question aggressively (as s. o. might question a speaker at a public meeting)

1. *What do you learn about Gabriel Conroy in this passage?*
2. *How does Miss Ivors differ from him?*
3. *Which of the two characters do you find more sympathetic? Why?*
4. *Miss Ivors was probably a member of the Gaelic League (→***H***, 1893). Say what you think of their aims. How important was this movement politically?*

The Home Rule Controversy

Ever since the Act of Union created the United Kingdom of Great Britain and Ireland in 1800, there had been movements to repeal it. Daniel O'Connell, who achieved Catholic Emancipation for the whole of the Kingdom in 1829 through a mixture of parliamentary work and popular agitation, tried to achieve "Repeal" through the same methods, but the resistance in this case was much greater.

The Great Famine (→**H**, 1846) changed the political scenery. Not only did it confirm Irish fears that a London administration would be insensitive to Irish needs, but it convinced many of the more enlightened English politicians that change was necessary.

In 1886 Liberal Prime Minister Gladstone introduced his first "Home Rule" bill in response to agitation by the Irish parliamentary leader Charles Stuart Parnell. This bill offered a devolution of certain powers to a Dublin parliament. Though much less than many radicals were demanding, it was enthusiastically received in Ireland, proving to many that England need no longer be seen as the national enemy. The bill was defeated in the House of Commons by a small majority.

The Conservative and aristocratic enemies of Home Rule either saw it as the first step towards dismantling the Empire, or complained that the safeguards for the minority interests of Protestants were insufficient. For the militant Protestants of the Ulster Orange Order (→**G**), the situation was clear: "Home Rule is Rome Rule".

The cultural revival that expressed itself in the formation of the Gaelic League in 1893 led to renewed demands for Home Rule. Gladstone's second bill passed the House of Commons this time, but was rejected in the House of Lords.

The third Home Rule bill of 1912 was met with threats of violence from Sir Edward Carson, leader of the Irish Unionist party. As the bill went backwards and forwards between the House of Commons and the House of Lords, the illegal Ulster Volunteer Force was established to resist its implementation. They were encouraged by an Army mutiny in early 1914: certain officers declared they would refuse to enforce Home Rule. In the meantime, the Great War had broken out.

The Bill received royal assent in September 1914, but its operation was suspended until after the war. When Carson and other Unionists were given high positions in a coalition government, many Irish nationalists began to doubt if it ever would be implemented. Events were to overtake them.

2 Catholicism, Protestantism and Politics

At the turn of the century, a strong socialist movement began to grow in Ireland, particularly in Dublin. Its spread in the more industrialized north was comparatively slow. Here, the Irish socialist leader James Connolly tries to explain why.

From time to time I propose to give some attention to the elucidation of the problems peculiar to Ireland and particularly to this part of it. For the present, it is sufficient to emphasise the fact that the religious affiliations of the population of Ulster determine their political leanings to a greater extent than is the case in any part of Europe outside the Balkans. But the manner in which this has developed is also unique. I believe that it is true to say that, politically speaking, the Protestantism of the North of Ireland has no parallel outside this country, and that the Catholicism of the Irish Catholics is, likewise, peculiar in its political trend.

To explain – I mean that, whereas, Protestantism has in general made for political freedom and political Radicalism, it has been opposed to slavish worship of kings and aristocrats. Here, in Ireland, the word Protestant is almost a convertible term with Toryism, lickspittle loyalty, servile worship of aristocracy and hatred of all that savours of genuine political independence on the part of the "lower classes."

And in the same manner, Catholicism which in most parts of Europe is synonymous with Toryism, lickspittle loyalty, servile worship of aristocracy and hatred of all that savours of genuine political independence on the part of the lower classes, in Ireland is almost synonymous with rebellious tendencies, zeal for democracy, and intense feelings of solidarity with all strivings upward of those who toil.

Such a curious phenomenon is easily understood by those who know the history of Ireland. Unfortunately for their spiritual welfare – and I am using the word "spiritual", not in its theological but in its better significance as controlling mental and moral development upward – the Protestant elements of Ireland were, in the main, plantation of strangers upon the soil from which the owners had been dispossessed by force. The economic dispossession was, perforce, accompanied by a political and social outlawry. Hence every attempt of the dispossessed to attain citizenship, to emerge from their state of outlawry, was easily represented as a tentative step towards reversing the plantation and towards replanting the Catholic and dispossessing the Protestant.

Imagine this state of matter persisting for over 200 years and one realises at once that the planted population – the Protestants – were bound to acquire insensibly a hatred of political reform and to look upon every effort

A Protestant anti-Home Rule poster.

of the Catholic to achieve political recognitions as a insidious move towards the expulsion of Protestants. Then the Protestant always saw that the kings and aristocrats of England and Ireland were opposed by the people whom he most feared and from recognising that it was but an easy step to regard his cause as identical with theirs. They had a common enemy, and he began to teach his children that they had a common cause, and common ideals.

This is the reason – their unfortunate isolation as strangers holding a conquered country in fee for rulers alien to its people – that the so-called Scotch of Ulster have fallen away from and developed antagonism to political reform and mental freedom as rapidly as the Scots of Scotland have advanced in adhesion to these ideals.

The Catholics, for their part, and be it understood I am talking only of the Catholic workers, have been as fortunately placed for their political education as they were unfortunately placed for their political and social condition. Just as the Socialist knows that the working class, being the lowest in the Social system, cannot emancipate itself without as a result emancipating all other classes, so the Irish Catholic has realised instinctively that he, being the most oppressed and disfranchised, could not win any modicum of political freedom or social recognition for himself without winning it for all others in Ireland. Every upward step of the Catholic has emancipated some one of the smaller Protestant sects; every successful revolt of the Catholic peasant has given some added security even to those Protestant farmers who were most zealously defending the landlord. And out of this struggle the Catholic has, perforce, learned toleration. He has learned that his struggle is, and has been, the struggle of all the lowly and dispossessed, and he has grown broadminded with the broadmindedness of the slave in revolt against slavery.

But with the advent of Home Rule, nay even with the promise of Home Rule and the entrance of Ireland upon the normal level of civilised, self-governing nations, the old relation of Protestant and Catholic begins to melt and dissolve, and with their dissolution will come a new change in the relation of either faith to politics. The loss of its privileged position will mean for Protestantism the possibilities of an immense spiritual uplifting; and emergence into a knowledge of its kinship with its brothers and sisters of different creeds. Whether the entrance of Catholicity into a position of mere numerical voting power will lead, in its turn, to a withering up of those kindly feelings born of its past sufferings is another matter. I do not believe that it will, at least amongst the toilers. Our apprenticeship to misery has been too long, our journeyings in the desert of slavery have surely implanted in our breasts a sense of the criminality of any attempt to impose fetters upon others such as we ourselves have worn. And out of that belief the writer looks forward with confidence to the future believing that the tale these Notes from Ireland will have to tell will be a hopeful one, even if the hope is nurtured amid storm and stress.

Article by James Connolly in *Forward*, May, 1913.

5 *elucidation* [ɪˌljuːsɪˈdeɪʃn] explanation – 8 *affiliation* state of belonging to a group – 9 *Ulster* the most northern of the four Irish provinces (→**G**) – 10 **leanings** tendencies, preferences – 15 *has no parallel* is without precedent or example – 24 *convertible term* synonym – *Toryism* the ideology of the British Conservative Party – *lickspittle* (coll.) servile (as of a person willing to lick s. o.'s boots) – 26 *to savour of* [ˈseɪvə] (fig.) to taste or smell of – 36 **zeal** enthusiasm, great desire to attain – 37 *strivings upward* attempts to improve their condition – 38 **to toil** to work – 48 **to dispossess** to deprive of one's possessions, esp. land – 49 *perforce* (lit.) by necessity – 50 *outlawry* the state of having been put outside the law – 53 *tentative* [ˈ–––] hesitant or experimental – 60 *were bound to acquire* unavoidably had to develop – 63 *insidious* treacherous or deceitful – **expulsion** expelling, driving out – 75 *in fee (for)* under the authority of a feudal lord – **alien** [ˈeɪljən] foreign – 76 *Scotch* (arch.) Scots (→**G**, Ulster Scots) – 77 **antagonism** [–ˈ–––] hostility – 79 *adhesion* [ædˈhiːʒn] act of holding fast to – 91 **to oppress** to keep down by force – *to disfranchise* to deprive of political rights – 92 *modicum (of)* small degree of s. th. – 97 **peasant** [ˈpezənt] poor farmer – 99 **zealously**

['zeləslı] with great zeal or enthusiasm – 100 **landlord** owner of land which is let to small farmers for rent – 103 **lowly** of low social status – 104 **broadminded** tolerant, free of prejudice or bigotry – 107 *advent* coming – *Home Rule* see Info Box p. 16 and →G – 114 **faith** here: religion – 117 *kinship* family belonging, brotherhood – 119 **creed** religion – 121 *withering up* dying (as of a cut plant) – 124 **apprenticeship** (fig.) position of a person who is learning a job from a master – 125 **misery** ['mızərı] great suffering – 128 *fetters* chains – 133 *to nurture* to protect and help to grow

1. *What, according to Connolly, is the typical political position of Protestants in most countries?*
2. *In what sense does he regard Irish Protestants as unfortunate, and Irish Catholics as fortunate?*
3. *How does he (indirectly) answer the charge "Home Rule is Rome Rule"?*

3 Ireland Unfree Shall Never Be at Peace

Though the 19th century was a time of political reforms, parliamentary campaigns and peaceful public agitation, the radical tradition had not died. Many believed that Britain would never concede independence unless to physical force. The militant Irish Republican Brotherhood (also called the Fenian movement) was founded simultaneously in Dublin and New York in 1858. The American branch consisted of people who had been forced to emigrate after the Famine, and they provided arms and military experience for a rising in 1867. Its failure was due to bad organization and the fact that many of the Fenians were already imprisoned.

After that the organization suspended its military activities and supported Home Rule – until the formation of the Ulster Volunteers in 1912 provided the signal for many of its members to take up arms again, calling themselves the Irish Volunteers. One of them was the schoolteacher and poet Pádraig (Patrick) Pearse. His ideas are most clearly expressed in this speech he delivered at the funeral of the Fenian leader Jeremiah O'Donovan Rossa, August 1, 1915.

It has seemed right, before we turn away from this place in which we have laid the mortal remains of O'Donovan Rossa, that one among us should, in the name of all, speak the praise of that valiant man, and endeavour to formulate the thought and the hope that are in us as we stand around his grave. And if there is anything that makes it fitting that I, rather than

What do these people want? (Consult the Chronology to find out more.)

some other, I rather than one of the grey-haired men who were young with him and shared in his labour and in his suffering, should speak here, it is perhaps that I may be taken as speaking on behalf of a new generation that has been rebaptised in the Fenian faith, and that has accepted the responsibility of carrying out the Fenian programme. I propose to you then that, here by the grave of this unrepentant Fenian, we renew our baptismal vows; that, here by the grave of this unconquered and unconquerable man, we ask of God, each one for himself, such unshakable purpose, such high and gallant courage, such unbreakable strength of soul as belonged to O'Donovan Rossa.

Deliberately here we avow ourselves, as he avowed himself in the dock, Irishmen of one allegiance only. We of the Irish Volunteers, and you others who are associated with us in today's task and duty, are bound together and must stand together henceforth in brotherly union for the achievement of the freedom of Ireland. And we know only one definition of freedom: it is Tone's definition, it is Mitchel's definition, it is Rossa's definition. Let no man blaspheme the cause that the dead generations of Ireland served by giving it any other name and definition than their name and their definition.

We stand at Rossa's grave not in sadness but rather in exaltation of spirit that it has been given to us to come thus into so close a communion with that brave and splendid Gael. Splendid and holy causes are served by men who are themselves splendid and holy. O'Donovan Rossa was splendid in the proud manhood of him, splendid in the heroic grace of him, splendid in the Gaelic strength and clarity and truth of him. And all that splendour and pride and strength was compatible with a humility and a simplicity of devotion to Ireland, to all that was olden and beautiful and Gaelic in Ireland, the holiness and simplicity of patriotism of a Michael O'Clery or of an Eoghan O'Growney. The clear true eyes of this man almost alone in his day visioned Ireland as we of to-day would surely have her: not free merely, but Gaelic as well; not Gaelic merely, but free as well.

In a closer spiritual communion with him now than ever before or perhaps ever again, in a spiritual communion with those of his day, living and dead, who suffered with him in English prisons, in communion of spirit too with our own dear comrades who suffer in English prisons to-day, and speaking on their behalf as well as our own, we pledge to Ireland our love, and we pledge to English rule in Ireland our hate. This is a place of peace, sacred to the dead, where men should speak with all charity and with all restraint; but I hold it a Christian thing, as O'Donovan Rossa held it, to hate evil, to hate untruth, to hate oppression, and hating them, to strive to overthrow them. Our foes are strong and wise and wary: but, strong and wise and wary as they are, they cannot undo the miracles of God who ripens in the hearts of young men the seeds sown by the young men of a former generation. And the seeds sown by the young men of '65 and '67 are coming to their miraculous ripening to-day. Rulers and Defenders of Realms had need to be wary if they would guard against such processes. Life springs from death; and from the graves of patriot men and women spring living nations. The Defenders of this Realm have worked well in secret and in the open. They think that they have pacified Ireland. They think that they have purchased half of us and intimidated the other half. They think that they have foreseen everything, think that they have provided against everything; but the fools, the fools, the fools! – they have left us our Fenian dead, and while Ireland holds these graves, Ireland unfree shall never be at peace.

3 **to concede** to grant, to allow – 4 *Fenian* [ˈfiːnjən] – 5 *the Famine* [ˈfæmɪn] →**H** – 8 *Home Rule, Ulster Volunteers* see Info Box p. 16 and →**G** – 14 **mortal** capable of dying – 15 *O'Donovan Rossa* (see introduction) – 17 *valiant* [ˈvæljənt] brave, heroic – **to endeavour** [ɪnˈdevə] to try – 20 **fitting** appropriate, suitable – 26 **to baptise** (fig.) to make part of a religious community by pouring water – 27 **faith** belief, religion – 30 **unrepentant** not regretting one's actions – 31 **vow** [vaʊ] solemn promise – 34 *gallant* heroic – 37 *to avow o.s.* to make a vow – 38 *the dock* place where the accused person stands in a court of law – 39 **alle-**

giance [əˈliːdʒəns] loyalty – *Irish Volunteers* see introduction and →**H**, 1913 – 42 *henceforth* from now on – 45 *Tone* see p. 12 and →**H**, 1798 – *Mitchel* John Mitchel, nationalist writer and member of the "Young Ireland" movement →**H**, 1848 – 52 *exaltation* [ˌeksɔːlˈteɪʃn] lifting up – 53 *communion* spiritual union – 54 **splendid** great – 55 *Gael* member of the Celtic Irish (Gaelic) people – **cause** ideal or goal of a group – 61 **compatible with** [–ˈ–––] in agreement with, capable of co-existing with – 63 *olden* (arch., lit.) in the old style – 65 *O'Clery, O'Growney* leaders of the Gaelic League →**H**, 1893 – 67 *to vision* [ˈvɪʒn] to see in a vision, to imagine – 78 **to pledge** to vow to give – 81 **sacred** [ˈseɪkrəd] holy – 85 **oppression** keeping down of a people by force – 86 **foe** enemy – 87 **wary** [ˈweərɪ] cautious, careful not to cause trouble – 89 **to ripen** to make ripe, to allow to grow – 92 *'65 and '67* dates of the Fenian risings (see introduction) – 98 *this Realm* [relm] British imperial rule – 100 **to pacify** to make peaceful – 101 **to intimidate** [–ˈ–––] to make afraid

1. *Explain what O'Donovan Rossa means to Pearse.*
2. *What has Pearse got in common with Wolfe Tone (l. 45)? Do their principles differ in any way?*
3. *Compare Pearse's concerns with those of Connolly (text II 3).*
4. *What do you think lines 97–99 refers to ("The Defenders of this Realm have worked well in secret and in the open.")?*
5. *Study the mystical and religious imagery used by Pearse.*
6. *In what way does Pearse acknowledge that the radicals were a tiny minority at the time?*

4 Easter 1916

"England's difficulty is Ireland's opportunity". This motto was put in practice in the middle of the Great War by a small band of Irish rebels in Dublin, including Pearse's Irish Volunteers and Connolly's Citizen Army. To the astonishment of a largely indifferent population, they managed to take and hold for a week several key buildings in the city. Due to conflicting orders, their supporters elsewhere in the country remained inactive, and the expected arms from Germany never arrived. Inevitably they had to surrender.

What changed the political landscape was not the rebellion but its aftermath, the execution of fifteen leaders and the imposition of martial law on the country. At the general election two years later, the militant republican party Sinn Féin won a landslide victory in Ireland, replacing the moderate Irish parliamentary party. The War of Independence broke out shortly afterwards.

The poet William Butler Yeats was acquainted with many of the 1916 rebel leaders. In this famous poem he reflects on what it all meant.

I have met them at close of day
Coming with vivid faces
From counter or desk among grey
Eighteenth-century houses.
I have passed with a nod of the head.
Or polite meaningless words,
Or have lingered awhile and said
Polite meaningless words,
And thought before I had done
Of a mocking tale or a gibe
To please a companion
Around the fire at the club,
Being certain that they and I
But lived where motley is worn:
All changed, changed utterly:
A terrible beauty is born.

That woman's days were spent
In ignorant good-will,
Her nights in argument
Until her voice grew shrill.
What voice more sweet than hers
When, young and beautiful,
She rode to harriers?
This man had kept a school
And rode our winged horse;
This other his helper and friend
Was coming into his force;

He might have won fame in the end,
So sensitive his nature seemed,
So daring and sweet his thought.
This other man I had dreamed
A drunken, vainglorious lout.
He had done most bitter wrong
To some who are near my heart,
Yet I number him in the song;
He, too, has resigned his part
In the casual comedy;
He, too, has been changed in his turn,
Transformed utterly:
A terrible beauty is born.

Hearts with one purpose alone
Through summer and winter seem
Enchanted to a stone
To trouble the living stream.
The horse that comes from the road,
The rider, the birds that range
From cloud to tumbling cloud,
Minute by minute they change;
A shadow of cloud on the stream
Changes minute by minute;
A horse-hoof slides on the brim,
And a horse plashes within it;
The long-legged moor-hens dive,
And hens to moor-cocks call;
Minute by minute they live:
The stone's in the midst of all.

Too long a sacrifice
Can make a stone of the heart.
O when may it suffice?
That is Heaven's part, our part
To murmur name upon name,
As a mother names her child
When sleep at last has come
On limbs that had run wild.
What is it but nightfall?
No, no, not night but death;
Was it needless death after all?
For England may keep faith
For all that is done and said.
We know their dream; enough
To know they dreamed and are dead;
And what if excess of love
Bewildered them till they died?
I write it out in a verse –
MacDonagh and MacBride
And Connolly and Pearse
Now and in time to be,
Wherever green is worn,
Are changed, changed utterly:
A terrible beauty is born.

Poem by William Butler Yeats,
September 25, 1916.

After the surrender of the rebels, Easter 1916.

Pearse, Irish Volunteers see text II 3 – *Connolly* see text II 2 – *Citizen Army* a group formed in 1913 to protect the workers in the general strike – *Sinn Féin* [ʃɪnˈfeɪn] →**G** – 2 **vivid** bright, lively – 7 **to linger** [ŋg] to wait for a while at or near a place – 10 *gibe* sarcastic expression – 14 *motley* dress of a jester, or court fool – *to wear motley* (fig.) to play the part of an entertainer – 15 **utterly** completely – 17 *that woman*... the Countess Constance Markievicz (née Gore-Booth), one of the leaders of the rebellion; sentenced to death, she was reprieved because of her sex – 23 *to ride to harriers* to go fox-hunting – 24 *this man*... Patrick Pearse – 25 *our winged horse* i. e. Pegasus, Greek mythological figure symbolizing poetic genius – 26 *this other* Thomas MacDonagh, another teacher and poet among the 1916 leaders – 27 *to come to one's force* to develop fully – 31 *this other man*... John MacBride, who married Maud Gonne, the woman Yeats was in love with – 32 *vainglorious* vain and pompous – **lout** [laʊt] stupid, uncultured person – 43 **to enchant** [enˈtʃɑːnt] to cast a magic spell on – 51 **brim** edge of s. th. – 53 *moor-hen* wild water-bird – 59 **to suffice** [səˈfaɪs] to be enough – 64 **limbs** here: legs – 68 **to keep faith** to keep one's promises – 78 *green* symbolic colour of Irish nationalism

1. *What was the poet's attitude to the rebels before the Easter rebellion?*
2. *What has been changed by the rebellion? What is Yeats' attitude to that change?*
3. *What doubts are expressed as to the wisdom of their act?*

Partition

The defeat of the 1916 Rising marked the beginning of the first really popular movement for total independence from Britain. Unfortunately, it ended in the partition of the country, a "solution" that satisfied nobody, but seemed to be the best that could be achieved. Besides, it was commonly seen as a temporary measure, something that could not last.

The partition of Ireland was based on the religious distribution of the population, since it was mainly Protestants who opposed Home Rule. According to the Treaty, a Boundary Commission was to adjust the border to the wishes of the local population. In fact it never took any action.

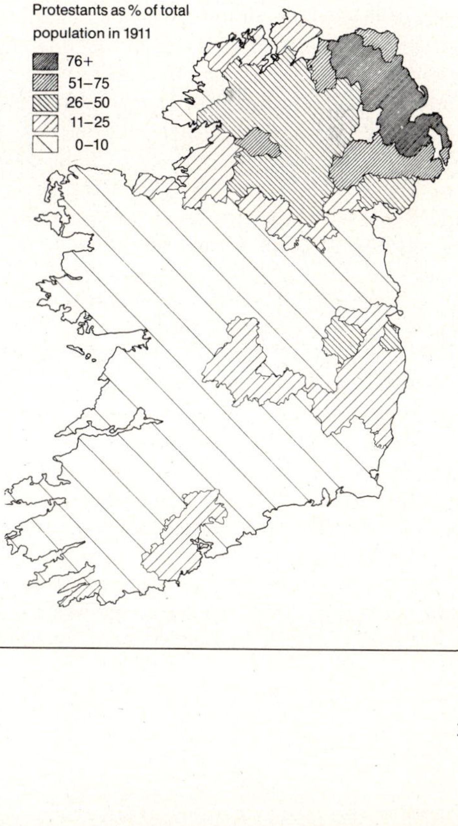

– *Examine the distribution shown on this map, and say in how many ways the border might have been drawn.*
– *Compare the actual border of Northern Ireland (inside front cover) with this map. What problems are to be expected?*

III The Troubled North

1 In Search of Ulster

The following was written in the late 1920s, when the partition of Ireland was something people still had to get used to. It is part of an account of a tour the English author made round the country, from Dublin to the south, then up the west coast to Donegal and across to Belfast.

When I said good-bye to Donegal I went south into Northern Ireland. An English reader who has not studied the map will wonder how I performed such an unnatural feat. It is simple.

Donegal, the most northerly county in Ireland and topographically in Ulster, is not in Northern Ireland! It is Free State territory. When the Irish Free State was established six of the nine counties of Ulster expressed themselves ready to die rather than become part of it. They decided to form themselves into a political entity with a parliament of their own. And this is Northern Ireland. [...]

As I went on into Northern Ireland a strange thing happened to me.

When I landed months ago in the Free State I adopted the attitude of foreigner in a foreign land. I had been, I hope, respectful, unargumentative, observant, anxious to understand and to be pleased. Now I realized as I went through towns and villages in Ulster that perhaps the boundary was not so nebulous as I had thought it. For I seemed to be in England again. There were war memorials quite as bad as those at home. I saw a Union Jack flying on a railway station. The pillar-boxes were red. The postmen were like English postmen. All trivial things, but after the Free State, which is trying to make itself as Irish as possible, they printed themselves on the mind with agreeable sharpness. In the South the deeds of the Irish troops in the Great War are never mentioned and no stone infantrymen remind one of the dead, but in Ulster every town and village is proud of the Ulster Division, and their war memorials stand beside the road as in towns and villages all over England, Scotland, and Wales. I had to look at the hills to convince myself that I had not, in some miraculous way, crossed the Irish Sea; but the hills were, beyond question, the hills of Ireland. [...]

Belfast is a great modern city with a population of 384,000. It is, even more so than Glasgow, a swift creation of the Industrial Revolution and the great expansion of Empire and trade that followed the eighteenth century. It is, like all modern cities, an eloquent tribute to the long start Great Britain once had over the rest of the world in the race for industrial supremacy. That time is now over and the rest of the world has caught up with us, hence many of the troubles of the Clyde and of the Belfast docks.

There is no grace about Belfast, as there is about Dublin. Belfast plays the Glasgow to Dublin's Edinburgh. Instead of grace and tradition Belfast has vigour and ambition. Dublin is feminine; Belfast is masculine. Could they marry, the child of their union would be a great and balanced nation. But the male is rather shy; he is afraid of losing his independence. He fears the woman. He thinks she might run up big bills and drag him into all kinds of unnecessary extravagance. She might also develop religious mania. He has therefore set up for himself a very expensive bachelor establishment; but – you never can tell! [...]

But the Belfast man [...] is, first of all, a perfectly comprehensible person, a staunch good fellow. He would never stab you in the back or forget you the instant you left the room. He prefers to praise rather than to blame. There is no malice in him. If he likes you he is your friend. If he dislikes you he says so, and there's an end of it. He is blunt, outspoken, and at times, even a bit crude. Loyalty to the Crown, and to the half-crown, is also a strong factor in

Shipbuilding – still Belfast's main industry.

his make-up. He enjoys power. He loves to make things. He has a great and unphilosophic pride in material achievement. He is not a Scotsman, as so many people consider him: he is a Calvinistic Irishman. The greatest of his qualities is perhaps honesty and reliability. He would never let you down...

Mrs. Dublin, dear, now that your *decree nisi* is pronounced – what a perfect husband!

From *In Search of Ireland* by H. V. Morton, London 1930. Reprinted from the 1984 Methuen edition, pp. 229–232, 251–253.

Ulster →**G** – 4 *Donegal* ['dʌnɪgɔːl] or [ˌ−−'−] – 7 **feat** difficult deed – 10 *Free State* →**G** – 15 *entity* unit – 21 *unargumentative* not causing trouble by arguing too much – 22 **observant** capable of noticing things – **anxious** wanting very much (to do s. th.) – 25 *nebulous* ['−−−] unreal, vague – 27 *war memorials* monuments to the dead of World War I – 28 **Union Jack** British flag – 29 *pillar-boxes... red* in the Irish Free State, the typical British round letter-boxes were immediately painted green – 35 *Great War* World War I – 36 *stone infantrymen* statues of soldiers – 48 **swift** quick – 51 **eloquent** ['−−−] (here fig.) able to speak well and expressively – 54 **supremacy** dominance, leadership – 56 *the Clyde* the Scottish river on which Glasgow is built – 57 **docks** harbour area – 58 **grace** beauty and style – 59 *plays the Glasgow to...* is more like Glasgow, whereas Dublin is more like the elegant city of Edinburgh – 61 **vigour** strength – 67 **to run up a bill** to buy recklessly and get in debt – 69 **mania** ['meɪnɪə] madness, exaggerated enthusiasm – 70 *bachelor establishment* dwelling for a single man – 73 **comprehensible** understandable – *staunch* [ɔː] steady, reliable – 74 *to stab s.o. in the back* (fig.) to harm s.o. secretly while pretending to be a friend – 77 **malice** ['−−] ill-feeling, hatred – 79 **blunt, outspoken** openly saying what one thinks – 80 **crude** primitive, too direct – *the Crown* the British monarchy – 81 *half-crown* a coin worth two shillings and sixpence (one eighth of a pound) in the old currency – 82 *his make-up* his character – 85 *not a Scotsman...* →**G**, Ulster Scots – 86 *Calvinistic* the Presbyterian religion widespread in Scotland and N. Ireland owes much to the teachings of Calvin – 89 *decree nisi* divorce

1. *Try to explain why Donegal and two other Ulster counties were allowed to become part of the Free State.*
2. *What outward signs tell the author that he is now back in the United Kingdom? What do these signs reveal about the political views of (most of) the inhabitants?*
3. *What additional factor (besides religion) has made the north-east of Ireland different from the rest of the country?*
4. *Describe the character of the typical Belfast loyalist.*
5. *Comment on the male-female imagery. How appropriate is it?*
6. *What is the author's opinion on the partition of Ireland?*

A Protestant State for a Protestant People?

The creation of two separate Irish states did not put an end to the violence. In the North, there were clashes between the illegal para-military groups IRA and UVF until order of a sort was imposed by the new police force, the Royal Ulster Constabulary, aided by the (later notorious) "B" Specials.

From the start, the one-third Catholic population had a very reserved attitude to the new state. They largely gave their votes to Nationalist politicians. Since the aim of these politicians was a united Irish Republic, they refused for many years to play the part of official opposition in the Stormont (Belfast) Parliament.

As a result, the ruling Unionists (who got their support from the two-thirds Protestant/loyalist section of the population) remained deeply suspicious of the Catholics. Many Unionists felt that Catholic "disloyalty" to the new state justified discrimination against them in many fields. In the 30s, several prominent Unionist politicians openly and defiantly declared their aim to be "a Protestant State/Parliament/Government... for a Protestant people". Thus was created a vicious circle of alienation and discrimination.

Gerrymandering: Since this term refers to the manipulation of (electoral) boundaries so as to secure an artificial majority, Northern Ireland itself can be seen as a gerrymandered state. Still, in spite of their built-in majority in the state as a whole, the Unionists continued to feel insecure, especially on the local level, and especially in the face of the higher Catholic birth-rate. The electoral boundaries of the city of Londonderry (Derry), constitute a classic example of gerrymandering. The city has a roughly two-to-one Catholic majority. Yet as late as 1967 the huge Catholic majority in one electoral district could elect only 8 representatives to the city council, whereas the small Protestant majorities in the two other districts elected a total of 12 Unionist members. (The British electoral system with its principle of winner-take-all made this possible.)

Other forms of discrimination: The effects of gerrymandering were made worse by the restriction of the vote in local elections to rate-payers (i. e. property owners). This amounted to a discrimination against the poor, who made up a larger proportion of the Catholics. Once in power, the Unionists had control of the allocation of council houses, and in many cases used this power to prevent any growth in Catholic influence. Employment was another field in which Catholics felt discriminated against.

What tradition are these Civil Rights demonstrators calling on?

The Civil Rights Movement: In spite of a brief IRA campaign in the fifties (abandoned because of lack of support), the post-war years were an era of relative peace. Rising living standards helped to soften people's attitudes on both sides. In 1963, Terence O'Neill became Prime Minister, with a programme of conciliation towards Catholics and friendship with the Republic of Ireland. In 1967 the Northern Ireland Civil Rights Association was formed (on the American model). Among their demands were electoral reform, fair housing allocation, and the abolition of the Protestant "B" Specials – i. e. not the old Nationalist call for the dissolution of the state, but just equal rights for all citizens within the state. A series of marches were held, some of which were attacked by extremist Protestants. A year later, many of their demands were met. But the price proved to be very high.

2 Making Sense of Civil Rights

Certain sections of the Protestant community reacted strongly – and sometimes violently – to the Civil Rights movement and to any concessions made by the O'Neill government. The following is an attempt to explain such reactions.

After all, the O'Neill era was a time of great hope and optimism for many people: most Protestants were feeling more, not less, conciliatory towards Catholics. The old entrenched attitudes seemed to be weakening on both sides and tolerance was visible: nuns could even be seen shopping in the most sacred pastures of loyalism, like the Shankill! […]

People were saying things were improving because Catholics were accepting the status quo, so proving there was nothing wrong with it; because Ulster was prospering as never before and because people were living and working together without any 'trouble'. So, they felt, why on earth should people want to make trouble now, when there was least reason for it?

Catholic leaders were not just taking part in state functions but Catholic were accepting cheerfully traditional Protestant expressions of feeling. So one group of East Belfast Orangemen recalled: 'One Catholic farmer used to look after his Protestant neighbour's cows on the 12th July, and everyone knew most ice cream sellers at the Field were Catholics.' As for the 11th and 12th celebrations,

Harmless tradition or provocation? – A 12th July Orange parade

they were just 'social occasions' where Catholics took their kids to watch the bonfires or parades. [...]

Parading through your own district also seemed not only natural to many people, but also tactful and respectful to the other side. So civil rights marchers who breached unspoken rules on territory in the name of nonsectarianism seemed deliberately aggressive. People would even appeal to 'outsiders' like myself for explanations: 'Look, say going through Antrim or some of those Protestant villages. They knew the political views of people there, so surely, it must have been just to stir them up? What other point could there have been (could you tell me?)' Thus the marchers were in an impossible dilemma: they were liable to be seen as sectarian whether or not they remained within Catholic areas.

The notion that Catholics were doing 'as well as they deserved' suggests some people saw discrimination as not just natural, but justified. [...]

Protestants in poorer areas of Belfast also expressed an exasperated gut feeling that if Catholics had a rough time, they must have asked for it, somehow. Protestants had a hard life too, but they didn't grumble, they 'went and looked for work'. if Catholics couldn't find work it must be because they didn't really want it. As this loyalist song expressed it:

And when their babies learn to talk
They shout 'discrimination' –
Their dad just lies in bed all day
And lives upon the nation.

All these arguments exempted the majority from blame, and put the onus for change on the minority.

So we can see that when the civil rights movement emerged, a few Protestants were prepared to make a leap of trust and accept that Protestants must change both their attitudes and their policies. A larger group felt Catholics could never be trusted, that their demands must be fought to the end. The rest were to varying degrees unwilling to accept that Protestants had any major responsibility for Catholic inequality, for past bitterness or future reconciliation. Civil rights offered them no proofs of Catholic loyalty, and challenged their definitions at every point by putting the blame squarely on the majority. The movement also said: 'You are not the sort of people you claim to be, fair and freedom loving: you are frauds or hypocrites.' People's definitions of themselves were fundamentally challenged.

In this situation people were likely to try and maintain their self image and integrity for as long as possible, and search all the harder for alternative explanations, especially as their own ideology did not give them the let-out of a proud admission: 'Yes, we discriminated and it was *right*'. Conspiracy theories gained wide circulation because they met the needs of many people at a particular time and reassured them that surely nice, contented Mrs Murphy down the road had nothing to do with this business:

'I've always thought there must be foreigners behind it all.'

'Things were going so well here that the Free State got worried support for the republicans would finally melt away. So they saw it as a last chance to stir up trouble and win the RCs back to the old cause.'

'The revolution is worldwide... Commies saying they were out for the people but really in it for themselves.' etc.

When political reforms did not bring peace but a devastating IRA campaign started after 1971, many Protestants felt their fears at this time had been vindicated, and that civil rights was indeed just an IRA front.

From *Ulster's Uncertain Defenders* by Sarah Nelson, Belfast: Appletree Press 1984, pp. 67–73.

2 *Civil Rights* see Info Box p. 26 – *O'Neill* Captain Terence O'Neill, moderate Unionist politician, Prime Minister of N. I. 1963–69 – 6 **conciliatory** willing to make concessions – 7 *entrenched* inflexibly hostile (like opposing armies in trenches) – 10 **sacred** ['seɪkrəd] holy – **pastures** fields for cattle; here fig.: home ground – 11 *loyalism* →**G** – *Shankill* [ʃæŋ'kɪl] Protestant working-class area of west Belfast – 15 **to prosper** to do well economically – 22 **functions** official ceremonies and social occasions – 25 *Orangemen* →**G** – 27 *the*

12th July see picture, p. 27 (also 12) – 31 **bonfire** large fire in the open air – 36 *to breach* to break (a rule) – 37 *nonsectarianism* the principle of not discriminating on account of religion – 40 *Look, say*… (coll.) Take as an example… – 51 **to justify** to make s. th. right – 54 *gut feeling* basic, instinctive reaction – 65 **to exempt** to free (s. o. from s. th.) – 66 *the onus* ['əʊnəs] the responsibility – 79 **to challenge** here: to demand to explain or justify – 84 **fraud** s. o. who lives by pretence – **hypocrite** ['hɪpəkrɪt] s. o. who professes high principles, etc., but does not really live by them – 90 *let-out* outlet, option – 101 *Free State* →**G** – *republicans* →**G** – 104 *RCs* Roman Catholics – 105 *commies* (sl.) communists – 109 **devastating** destructive, catastrophic – *IRA* →**G** – 111 **to vindicate** to prove right

1. *Why were many Protestants suspicious of Catholic demands for civil rights?*
2. *What were Protestant-Catholic relations like before the Civil Rights movement?*
3. *What connection was seen between traditional Orange parades and the Civil Rights marches?*
4. *What alternative explanations did some Protestants find for the Civil Rights movement?*

3 After the March

In August 1969 the British Army was brought in to keep the peace, after a number of clashes between Civil Rights demonstrators and militant Protestants. At first the troops were welcomed by the Catholics, but this changed when it seemed they were being used to help the police suppress Civil Rights activities. This is the background for Brian Friel's play The Freedom of the City.

In this play, which is set in Derry, three people believed to be armed terrorists are shot by British soldiers when trying to surrender. The following extract from Act I shows how it all began – with a crowd of people running away from police and troops after a banned Civil Rights march has been broken up. Three of them find shelter in a nearby building…

SKINNER: Hi! Missus! There's a place up here!

LILY: Where?

SKINNER: Up here! Come on! Quick! Quick!

LILY: Give me a hand, young fella. You'll have to lead me.

(*He runs down to her, grabs her arm, and drags her roughly upstage.*)

SKINNER: Come on – come on – come on! Move, will you! Move:

LILY: No need to pull the arm off me.

SKINNER: Did you get a dose of the CS gas?

LILY: D'you think I'm playing blind-man's-buff? God, you're a rough young fella, too.

SKINNER: In here. Quick. Watch the step.

LILY: My good coat! Mother of God, will you watch my good coat!

SKINNER: I should have left you to the soldiers.

LILY: They'd be no thicker nor you.

SKINNER: D'you want to go back to them, then?

LILY: Don't be so damned smart.

SKINNER: There's a chair behind you.

LILY: I can manage myself.

(*She drops into a chair and covers her face with both hands.*)

LILY: O my God, that's sore on the eyes. There's someone else back there.

SKINNER: Where!

LILY: Just outside.

(SKINNER *rushes out of the room.*)

LILY: Where's this, young fella? Whose house is this?

(SKINNER *finds* MICHAEL *on his hands and knees and gets down beside him.*)

SKINNER: Come on! Get up! They're going wild out there!

(MICHAEL *groans.*)

SKINNER: Are you hurt? Did you get a rubber bullet?

MICHAEL: Gas.

SKINNER: You're okay. Come on. You can't lie here. Can you walk?

MICHAEL: Leave me.

(*Sudden burst of rubber bullets, followed by screaming and the revving of armoured vehicles.* SKINNER *lies flat on his face until the burst is over. Then he suddenly grabs* MICHAEL *by the back of his jacket and drags him, face down and limp, up to the door and into the parlour. He drops him in the middle of the room, runs back to the door, locks it. As they enter,* LILY *uncovers her eyes momentarily.*)

LILY: I just thought it was a young fella. Is he hurted bad?

(*After locking the door,* SKINNER *moves around the room, examining it with quick, lithe efficiency.*)

SKINNER: No.

LILY: (*To* MICHAEL) Did you get a thump of a baton, young fella?

SKINNER: Gas.

LILY: Maybe he got a rubber bullet in the stomach.

SKINNER: Only gas.

LILY: He might be bleeding internal.

SKINNER: Gas! Are you deaf?

LILY: I like to see the blood. As long as you can see the blood there's always hope.

SKINNER: He'll come round.

LILY: I seen a polisman split a young fella with a baton one Saturday evening on Shipquay Street. His head opened like an orange and the blood spurted straight up – you know like them pictures you see of whales, only it was red. And at twelve Mass the next day who was sitting in the seat in front of me but your man, fresh as a bap, and the neatest wee plaster from here to here, and him as proud of his-self.

(MICHAEL *gets himself into a sitting position on the floor.*)

MICHAEL: Aaaaagh.

LILY: Are you all right, young fella?

MICHAEL: I think so.

LILY: (*To* SKINNER) I was afeard by the way he was twisting, the kidneys was lacerated.

MICHAEL: That's desperate stuff.

LILY: It's a help if you cross your legs and breathe shalla.

MICHAEL: God – that's awful.

LILY: Did you walk into it or what?

MICHAEL: A canister burst right at my feet.

LILY: You should have threw your jacket over it. They come on us very sudden, didn't they?

MICHAEL: I don't know what happened.

LILY: What got into them anyway?

SKINNER: Did no one tell you the march was banned?

LILY: I knew the march was banned.

SKINNER: Did you expect them to give you tea at the end of it?

LILY: I didn't expect them to drive their tanks through us and shoot gas and rubber bullets into us, young fella. It's a mercy to God if no

5 *Derry* second-largest city in N. I., officially (but not popularly) known as Londonderry – 9 *Missus* = Mrs – 12 *fella* = fellow – 15 *upstage* to the back of the stage – 19 **dose** the required (medical) amount of s. th. – *CS gas* a kind of tear gas – 20 *blind man's buff* a game in which one person is blindfolded and has to chase the others – 27 *no thicker nor* (dial.) no stupider than – 29 **smart** here: clever in an unpleasant way – 53 *revving* (from "to rev up") the sound of a vehicle starting up – 57 **limp** hanging loosely, with no strength – 64 *lithe* [laɪð] smoothly moving – **efficiency** the ability to do s. th. well – 67 *to get a thump of* to be hit by s. th. hard – 68 *baton* [ˈbætn] here: the short, heavy stick carried by an otherwise unarmed police officer – 74 **deaf** [e] unable to hear – 77 **to come round** to recover consciousness – 78 *polisman* [ˈ–––] (dial.) policeman – 85 *bap* (dial.) baby – *wee* (dial.) little – 92 *afeard* (dial.) afraid – 93 *kidney* an internal organ – *to lacerate* to tear, to damage badly – 94 *desperate* here coll.: terrible – 96 *shalla* = shallow – 105 **to ban s. th.** to order that s. th. should not take place

one's hurted. (*To* MICHAEL) Where were you standing?

MICHAEL: Beside the platform. Just below the speakers.

LILY: I was at the back of the crowd, beside wee Johnny Duffy – you know – the window-cleaner – Johnny the Tumbler – and I'm, telling him what the speakers is saying 'cos he hears hardly anything now since he fell off the ladder the last time. And I'm just after telling him 'The streets is ours and nobody's going to move us' when I turn round and Jesus, Mary and Joseph there's this big Saracen right behind me.

Of course I took to my heels. And when I look back there's Johnny the Tumbler standing there with his fists in the air and him shouting, 'The streets is ours and nobody's going to move us!' And you could hardly see him below the Saracen. Lord, the chairman'll enjoy that.

(MICHAEL *gets to his feet and sits in the chair.*)

LILY: Are you better?

MICHAEL: I'm all right.

LILY: Maybe you concussed yourself when you fell. If you feel yourself getting drowsy, shout 'Help! Help!'

MICHAEL: I'm fine.

LILY: D'you know what they say? That CS gas is a sure cure for stuttering. Would you believe that, young fella? That's why Celia Cunningham across from us drags her wee Colm Damien into the thick of every riot from here to Strabane and him not seven till next May.

(MICHAEL *coughs again. She offers him a handkerchief.*)

LILY: Here.

MICHAEL: Thanks.

LILY: Cough hard.

MICHAEL: I'm fine.

LILY: If you don't get it up, it seeps down through the lungs and into the corpuscles.

MICHAEL: I'm over the worst of it.

LILY: Every civil rights march Minnie McLaughlin goes on – she's the floor above me – she wears a miraculous medal pinned on her vest. Swears to God it's better nor a gas-mask.

(MICHAEL *chokes again, almost retches.*)

LILY: Good on you, young fella. Keep it rising. Anyways last Wednesday week Minnie got hit on the leg with a rubber bullet and now she pretends she has a limp and the young fellas call her Ché Guevara. If God hasn't said it, she'll be looking for a pension from the Dublin crowd.

(SKINNER*'s inspection is now complete – and he realizes where he is. He bursts into sudden laughter – a mixture of delight and excitement and malice.*)

SKINNER: Haaaaaaaaah!

(*Still laughing, he races right round the room, pounds on the door with his fists, runs downstage and does a somersault across the table.*)

LILY: Jesus, Mary and Joseph!

SKINNER: Haaaaaaaah!

LILY: The young fella's a patent lunatic!

SKINNER: Haaaaaaah!

LILY: Keep away from me, young fella!

(SKINNER *stops suddenly beside her and puts his face up to hers.*)

SKINNER: Do you know where you are, Missus?

LILY: Just you lay one finger on me!

SKINNER: Do you know where you're sitting!

LILY: I'm warning you!

SKINNER: Look around – look around – look around.

(*To* MICHAEL) Where are you? Where do you find yourself this Saturday afternoon? (*To*

114 **platform** raised stage for public speakers – 119 *'cos* = because – 121 *I'm just after telling…* (dial.) I have just told… – 124 *Saracen* a kind of armoured car (tank-like military vehicle) – 131 *chairman* presumably, the chairman of the local Civil Rights committee – 135 *concussed* suffering from concussion, i. e. the effect on the brain of a heavy blow on the head – 136 **drowsy** [ˈdraʊzɪ] sleepy – 143 **riot** violent demonstration – 144 *Strabane* [strəˈbæn] town about 15 miles south of Derry – 151 **to seep** (of a liquid or gas) to move slowly through s. th. – 152 *corpuscles* blood cells – 156 *miraculous medal* medal with a figure of the Virgin Mary, believed by some Catholics to have the power to cause miracles – 157 *vest* here: a garment worn next to the skin – 163 **to have a limp** to walk irregularly because of an injured or deformed leg – 164 *Ché Guevara* South American revolutionary leader – 165 **pension** regular payment to s. o. who can no longer work – *the Dublin crowd* the Government of the Irish Republic – 170 **malice** [ˈ––] the wish to do s. th. bad – 174 **somersault** acrobatic jump, turning completely head over heels – 177 *a patent lunatic* crazy

both) Guess – come on – guess – guess – guess. Ten-to-one you'll never hit it. Fifty-to-one. A hundred-to-one.

MICHAEL: Where?

SKINNER: Where, Missus, where?

LILY: How would I know?

SKINNER: I'll tell you where you are.

MICHAEL: Where?

SKINNER: You. Are. Inside. The Guildhall.

LILY: We are not!

SKINNER: In fact you're in the Mayor's parlour.

LILY: You're a liar!

SKINNER: The holy of holies itself!

LILY: Have a bit of sense, young fella. What would we be doing in –?

SKINNER: Look around! Look around!

MICHAEL: How did we get in?

SKINNER: By the side door.

MICHAEL: It's always guarded.

SKINNER: The soldiers must have moved into the Square to break up the meeting. (*To* LILY) When the trouble started you must have run down Guildhall Street.

LILY: How would I know where I run. I followed the crowd.

SKINNER: (*To* MICHAEL) You did the same.

MICHAEL: After the canister burst I don't know what happened.

LILY: So we just walked in?

SKINNER: By the side door and along the corridor and in here. Into the private parlour of His Worship, the Lord Mayor of Derry. (*He flings a cushion at the wall.*) Yipeeeeeeee!

(LILY *stands up.* MICHAEL *stands up. They stare in awe at their surroundings. As they gaze: A* SOLDIER *crouches at the very edge of stage right and speaks into his portable radio. His message is received by a* SOLDIER *at the very edge of stage left.*)

SOLDIER 1: Blue Star to Eagle. Blue Star to Eagle.

SOLDIER 2: Eagle receiving. Come in, Blue Star.

SOLDIER 1: The fucking yobbos are inside the fucking Guildhall!

SOLDIER 2: Jesus!

SOLDIER 1: What the fuck am I supposed to do?

SOLDIER 2: How did they get in?

SOLDIER 1: On fucking roller skates – how would I know!

SOLDIER 2: How many of them?

SOLDIER 1: No idea. The side door's wide open.

SOLDIER 2: What's your position, Blue Star?

SOLDIER 1: Guildhall Street. At the junction of the quay. What am I to do?

SOLDIER 2: Hold that position.

SOLDIER 1: Fucking great! For how long?

SOLDIER 2: Until you're reinforced.

SOLDIER 1: Thanks, mate!

SOLDIER 2: Do not attempt to enter or engage.

SOLDIER 1: Okay.

SOLDIER 2: I'll get back to you in a few minutes.

(*They go off.*
A television newsman, LIAM O'KELLY, *appears on one of the battlements. Into a microphone:*)

O'KELLY: I am standing on the walls overlooking Guildhall Square in Derry where only a short time ago a civil rights meeting, estimated at about three thousand strong, was broken up by a large contingent of police and troops. There are no reports of serious casualties but unconfirmed reports are coming in that a group of about fifty armed gunmen have taken possession of the Guildhall here below me and have barricaded themselves in. If the reports are accurate, and if the Guildhall, regarded by the minority as a symbol of Unionist domination, has fallen into the hands of the terrorists, both the security forces and the Stormont government will be acutely

198 *the Guildhall* the city hall of Londonderry – 200 **parlour** sitting room – 233 *fucking, the fuck* (vulg.) here, meaningless expletives – *yobbos* (sl., derog.) uncultured people – 244 **junction** where two or more streets meet – 245 **quay** [kiː] waterfront (here, of the River Foyle) – 248 *to reinforce* here: to bring in more soldiers – 250 *to engage* here: to start a military engagement, i. e. fight – 256 *battlements* town walls, once built for military protection – 261 **contingent** [kənˈtɪndʒənt] – 262 **casualties** injuries or deaths – 266 **to barricade o. s. in** to build barriers around o. s., so that one cannot be attacked – 268 *the minority* here: the Catholic community, a minority in N. I., though a majority in Derry – 269 *Unionist domination, Stormont* see Info Box p. 26 and →**G** – 271 *Stormont* location of the N. I. Government in Belfast

embarrassed. Brigadier Johnson-Hansbury who was in charge of today's elaborate security operation has, so far, refused to confirm or deny the report. No comment either from the Chief Superintendent of Derry's Royal Ulster Constabulary. But usually reliable spokesmen from the Bogside insist that the story is accurate, and already small groups are gathering at street corners within the ghetto area to celebrate, as one of them put it to me, 'the fall of the Bastille'. This is Liam O'Kelly returning you to our studios in Dublin.

(*As he finishes, a man enters left – the* BALLADEER. *A glass in one hand, a bottle in the other. He is unsteady on his feet but his aggressive jubilance makes him articulate. Dressed in shirt and trousers; the shirt dirty and hanging over the trousers. As he swaggers across the stage he is followed by an* ACCORDIONIST *and a group of dancing* CHILDREN. *He sings, to the air of John Brown's Body.*)

BALLADEER: A hundred Irish heroes one February day
Took over Derry's Guildhall, beside old Derry's quay.
They defied the British army, they defied the RUC,
They showed the crumbling empire what good Irishmen could be.

(*The* CHILDREN *join in the chorus:*)

CHILDREN: Three cheers and then three cheers again for Ireland one and free,
For civil rights and unity, Tone, Pearse and Connolly.
The Mayor of Derry City is an Irishman once more,
So let's celebrate our victory and let Irish whiskey pour.

BALLADEER: The British Army leader was a gentle English lad;
If he beat those dirty Paddys they might make him a lord.
So he whispered to his Tommies, 'Fix them, chaps; I'll see you right!'
But the lads inside the Guildhall shouted back 'Come on and fight!'

TOGETHER: Three cheers and then three cheers again for Ireland one and free,
For civil rights and unity, Tone, Pearse and Connolly.
The Mayor of Derry City is an Irishman once more,
So let's celebrate our victory and let Irish whiskey pour.

(*They go off right.*

MICHAEL *begins to move around the parlour, silently, deferentially.* LILY *stand very still; only her eyes move.* SKINNER *watches her closely. Pause.*

MICHAEL: Christ Almighty – the Mayor's parlour!

(*Silence.*)

From *The Freedom of the City* by Brian Friel, London: Faber 1974, pp. 22–30.

272 **to embarrass** to put s. o. in an awkward position – 273 **elaborate** [ɪˈlæbərɪt] very extensive – 276 *Royal Ulster Constabulary* →**G** (RUC) – 278 *Bogside* Catholic working-class district of Derry – 285 *balladeer* singer of ballads – 288 **jubilance** feeling of joy and triumph – **articulate** [ɑːˈtɪkjʊlɪt] able to express o. s. – 290 **to swagger** to walk in a showy, self-important manner – 298 **to defy** to resist – 305 *Tone, Pearse, Connolly* Irish rebel heroes; see pp. 12, 19/21 and 17/21 respectively – 313 *Paddy (Br. sl.) Irishman (from the short form of "Patrick")* – 315 *Tommy* (sl.) British soldier – 316 **chaps** (Br. coll.), **lads** (Ir. coll.) fellows – 329 *deferentially* with a feeling of respect

1. *Describe how Lily, Skinner and Michael come together.*
2. *Which of the three main characters do you get to know best here? Why?*
3. *How much is revealed here about their reasons for taking part in the civil rights march?*
4. *What do the outsiders think is happening? How far from the truth is this?*
5. *Compare the attitudes of the British soldiers, the TV newsman and the ballad-singers to what they think is happening.*
6. *How could the taking of the Derry's city hall be compared to "the fall of the Bastille" (l. 282)? (Consider the political background given in the Info Box, p. 26.)*
7. *Lily uses a lot of dialect forms and non-standard grammar. Find examples of both.*

4 Just Carrying out an Operation

From 1970 on, the IRA had become active again, and were soon waging full-scale war on what they saw as the British occupation troops. Though responsible for numerous atrocities – bombings and shootings which left large numbers of civilians as well as soldiers and police officers dead or maimed – they continued to enjoy the support of a sizeable section of the Catholic community. And no matter what measures were taken to suppress them, they have never had any trouble recruiting new members.

One who joined as a teenager in the early seventies was Mairead Farrell. For her part in the bombing of a Belfast hotel she spent ten years in jail. Here is part of the story she told to journalist Jenny McGeever shortly after her release.

Mairead Farrell was already in a cell in Dunmurry police station when she heard the three bombs go off in Conway's Hotel a few hundred yards up the road. The last she had seen of the other two volunteers was when she had been running away from the hotel grounds after the three of them had planted the bombs. They had been running in the opposite direction as police convoys had surrounded the hotel.

It was now about two hours later and she had been caught. She didn't yet know that one volunteer had been shot dead at point blank range while trying to escape from the police cordon.

There had been a lot of IRA activity throughout the North that day, Monday, April 5, 1976. A UDR man was shot dead in Armagh, and there were nine bombings – five of these in Belfast. It was just over a month since the withdrawal of political status in the North's jails and the IRA was carrying out a large number of operations – bombings and shootings – in protest against this.

Mairead Farrell, Sean McDermott and Kieron Doherty made their way around lunchtime that day to Conway's Hotel in Dunmurry to carry out one of these operations. The suitcase they carried contained three five-pound bombs, which were to be placed in the hotel – one upstairs, one in the dining-room and one in the lounge. Farrell and McDermott carried colt 45's and Doherty, a magnum pistol. The hotel had been designated a "political and economic target" by the IRA and was also frequented by members of the security forces.

The three burst into the wooden security hut, surrounded with wire mesh, at the entrance to the hotel and ordered the two security men there to lie down on the floor. Kieron Doherty remained with them while the other two went into the hotel, bringing with them a security woman, who was at the door. They ordered everyone in the hotel to lie down, planted the three bombs saying they were from the Irish Republican Army, shouted a warning, telling everyone that they had time to get out. And then they ran.

Mairead Farrell recalls that there were quite a few people in the hotel at the time. But there had been no panic. Everyone had been cooperative and no one had been hurt.

She had just got into a car in the hotel grounds when Sean McDermott shouted: "Mairead, it's the cops, run." She got out of the car as a police van pulled up alongside her. She ran towards the swimming pool in the hotel grounds, dropping her bag and colt 45 as she ran. The next voice she heard said "halt or we'll shoot." The police officer caught her and shoved her into the back of a police car, which drove off. She thinks that somebody had alerted the police or "tipped a bell somewhere along the way."

The police drove her to a house somewhere in the immediate vicinity. She didn't know why she had been brought there. There were plain clothes detectives all around the house and an ambulance was parked outside. A branch man came over to her in the car and asked her "how many are there?" She replied she didn't know what they were talking about. The detective countered "we've got them held up in the house," and she gave the same reply as earlier. She remembers that they stayed outside the house for about thirty minutes.

In the cell at Dunmurry, she had started getting anxious. A detective asked her did she know Sean McDermott and she gave her standard reply that she didn't know what they were talking about. The detective told her McDermott was dead. She didn't believe it. She remembers thinking they were trying to "fool her" to get information. It was about an hour later when they brought her a tape recorder of a news bulletin, a radio, a copy of the *Belfast Telegraph* and the photograph of a man lying bloody and dead on a pavement. [...]

She had spent her three days in custody in Dunmurry police station, thinking about Sean. She had liked him a lot. He had been her friend. [...] They gave her food but she couldn't eat it. "I was still weighing up could it be true. I knew I suppose it must be, from the cops' photo of him lying dead. It was really awful, thinking of him dead."

She'd also read in the papers by now there had been no injuries at Conway's when the three bombs went off. "It was never our intention to kill anyone. That's why we gave the warning. Hotels were political and economic targets during the political status arguments. I was just carrying out an operation."

Does she regret her part in the Conway Hotel bombings?

"Jesus, no. I went out on an operation and there was the possibility of my being killed or caught. It's just one of those things. I did ten and a half for that. There's no point in crying over it now."

Mairead doesn't regret the ten and a half years either... "No, it was worth it because I went out on the operation. There's no regrets... except that I got caught."

From "The Story of Mairead Farrell" by Jenny McGeever in *Magill*, Dublin, October 1986, pp. 8–9.

7 *Mairead* [mɔːˈreːd] Gaelic form of "Margaret" – 11 *Dunmurry* suburb of Belfast – 14 *volunteers* here: IRA activists – 18 **convoy** a number of vehicles travelling together – 22 *at point blank range* from very close – 24 *cordon* circle formed by police – 25 *IRA, UDR* →**G** – 28 *Armagh* town and county south-west of Belfast – 30 *withdrawal of political status* previous to March 1, 1976, IRA prisoners were in a "special category", kept separate from ordinary criminals (also →**H**, 1981) – 34 *Sean* [ʃɔːn] – *Kieron* [ˈkiːrən, ˈkiːrɔːn] 47 *wire mesh* a fence made of woven wire – 61 **to be cooperative** here: to do what was asked – 64 **cops** (sl.) police – 72 **to alert** to inform, to warn – 75 *in the vicinity* nearby – 77 *plain clothes* in ordinary civilian clothes, not in uniform – 93 **to fool s.o.** to play a trick on s.o. – 95 **news bulletin** short news broadcast – 103 *to weigh up* to consider possibilities

1. *What was the IRA's purpose in bombing the Conway Hotel?*
2. *Describe how the three "volunteers" carried out the "operation". What went wrong for them?*
3. *Discuss Mairead Farrell's attitude to the bombing – and to her ten years in prison.*
4. *No one was hurt in the Conway bombing, but this is certainly not the rule. How would the IRA justify*
   a) *the deliberate killing of soldiers and police?*
   b) *the frequent accidental killing of innocent civilians?*

The Death Toll

The death toll of the 20 years of "troubles" to the end of 1988 has been 2,711. This table shows how many people were killed each year. Indicated separately are the army and police deaths, almost all caused by the IRA. The rest includes UVF and UDA killings, purely sectarian murders, terrorist "mistakes" and "own goals", and killings by the security forces.

– *Try to relate these death statistics to the events listed in the Chronology on pp. 7–8.*

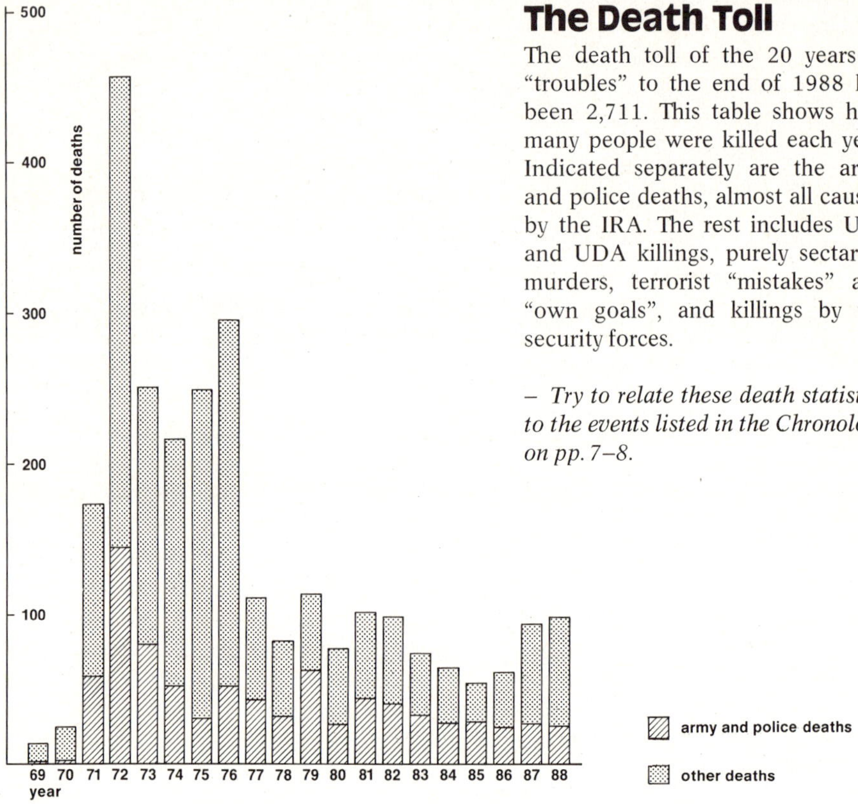

5 The South African Parallel

Irish bishops defeated in vote on violence

Tutu argues understanding of force as last resort

These headlines refer to the controversy caused in 1988 when the Anglican Bishops' Conference passed a resolution that seemed to justify violence in certain circumstances. Here are two clearly opposed views.

THE IRISH TIMES

13 D'OLIER STREET, DUBLIN 2
FRIDAY, AUGUST 5, 1988

THE USE OF VIOLENCE

"This conference . . . understands those who, after exhausting all other ways, choose the way of armed struggle as the only way to justice, whilst drawing attention to the dangers and injustices possible in such actions."

This sentence in the resolution on war, violence and justice, which was adopted by the Lambeth Conference yesterday, cannot but provoke controversy in a country where so many have died at the hands of those who claim to have chosen armed struggle as the only way to justice.

But for Irish paramilitaries of any hue either to seek consolation or to attempt to justify their actions by reference to the bishops' decision would be to add yet another layer of hypocrisy to the obscenity of their crimes. It would also be to diminish and distort the case made for the resolution and for his people in South Africa by Archbishop Desmond Tutu.

"Our people," said Dr Tutu, "have used conventional, non-violent methods and each time there has been a violent response on the part of those our people were seeking to persuade . . . We are saying that there are those of our people who are saying that we have tried everything. And we say we understand."

Some have sought to compare conditions in Northern Ireland with those in South Africa. Despite the many grievances of the Northern minority, there is no serious comparison. The institutional injustice of apartheid alone makes South Africa unique; and it is now reinforced by the systematic blocking of virtually every avenue of democratic opposition.

* * *

At his party's ard fheis on November 2nd, 1981, Mr Danny Morrison of Sinn Fein said: "Will anyone here object if, with a ballot paper in this hand and an Armalite in this hand, we take power in Ireland?" Dr Tutu's people do not have ballot papers in their hands. The people of Northern Ireland do; however impatient or frustrated some of them may feel, they have not exhausted the democratic means of redress.

There are other crucial distinctions: Dr Tutu represents a majority of the people in South Africa; the Irish paramilitaries do not have the support of a majority in Northern Ireland, in the Republic, or in the island as a whole. As the Bishop of Clogher, Dr Brian Hannon, put it: "The armed stuggle in our country has been totally counter-productive and is simply leading us further and further into depravity, amorality and violence."

Editorial in *The Irish Times*, Dublin, August 5, 1988.

2 **to exhaust** here: to try and fail, to use up (another option) – 7 *Lambeth* [ˈ––] district of London which contains the main residence of the Archbishop of Canterbury – 8 *cannot but* must – 12 *hue* colour; here fig.: political views – 13 **consolation** the lessening of troubles, worry, grief, etc. – 15 **layer** a thickness of some material placed over a surface – **hypocrisy** [hɪˈpɒkrɪsɪ] dishonest show of feeling – 16 **to diminish** to lessen – **to distort** to twist the meaning of – 18 *Desmond Tutu* Anglican Archbishop of Cape Town and winner of Nobel Peace Prize in 1984 – 22 **to persuade** to talk to s. o. and make them agree – 27 **grievance** strong complaint, s. th. which makes s. o. angry – *minority* here: Catholic community – 29 *apartheid* the South African policy of racial separation – **unique** the only one of its kind – 30 **to reinforce** [ˌ––ˈ–] to make stronger – 31 *avenue* here: option – 32 *ard fheis* [ˈɔːrdˌeʃ] (Gael.) party conference – 33 *Sinn Fein* →**G** – 34 **ballot paper** voting paper – 35 *Armalite* a kind of machine gun – 39 *redress* the setting right of a wrong – 40 **crucial** very important – 44 *Clogher* [ˈklɒhə(r)] town and Anglican diocese in the Republic of Ireland – 47 **depravity** [dɪˈprævɪtɪ] total moral badness – *amorality* [ˌeɪməˈrælɪtɪ] lack of morals

Parallel with S. Africa closer than we imagine

We may permit ourselves a smile as the Lambeth Conference squirms to find a formula that condemns armed struggle in Northern Ireland while approving it in South Africa. The familiar distinctions between democratic and undemocratic systems and between struggles for majority rights and minority rights are trotted out. Perhaps we should ask where these neat distinctions would go if Eugene Terreblanche's party ever achieved their goal of a white Boer Republic. What happens when partition by force after a civil war creates an artificial Afrikaner state with a white majority (and the lion's share of the wealth and industry)? Do all good English liberals then become supporters of self-determination for the "democratic majority" in the artificial Afrikaner state, and condemn as murdering terrorists those seeking to reunify the country?

The parallels between South Africa and Ireland are closer than the bishops imagine. It is simply that in Ireland the artificial settlers' state has already been created – by the artificial border drawn in 1922 by the colonial power against the will of the majority of Irishmen, and for the sole purpose of preventing the Ulster settlers coming under native rule. If France had done that in Algeria, conserving an artificial enclave with a French settler majority, would it be tolerated by Algerians today? Would the liberal world support "self-determination" for the French settler enclave? Curious how English liberals can perceive where historic justice lies in the case of Africans and Arabs, but not in the case of Irishmen.

Mike Crowe,
Geneva, Switzerland.

Letter to the editor, *The Guardian Weekly*, London, September 4, 1988.

2 **to squirm** to twist around in pain or discomfort – 3 **to condemn** to say s.th. is bad, to express disapproval of – 8 *to trot out* (coll.) to present – 9 **neat** tidy – 10 *Eugene Terreblanche* leader of the South African far-right-wing Afrikaner Resistance Movement – 12 *Boer* Afrikaner, i.e. white South African of Dutch descent – 13 **partition** the division of a country into two or more parts – 17 **self-determination** the right of the people of a country to decide their own affairs (by majority vote) – 21 **to reunify** to unite again – 26 *border drawn in 1922* →**H** – 37 **to perceive** to see

1. *Why were the Irish bishops opposed to the resolution on violence?*
2. *How does The Irish Times answer their worries? List their arguments.*
3. *What are the arguments for a parallel with the South African situation?*
4. *Is it only "English liberals" (letter, l. 36) who reject violence in Northern Ireland?*
5. *Group work: Prepare a debate on the topic. Use the information given elsewhere in this book to support or refute the various arguments.*

6 A British Cop in Northern Ireland

In 1984 John Stalker, a high-ranking Manchester policeman, was asked to set up an enquiry into the killings of six people by the Royal Ulster Constabulary. Their deaths had given rise to speculation that the RUC (as well as the army and the SAS) had a "shoot-to-kill" policy against suspected IRA terrorists.

Two years later, just as he was finishing his task, Stalker was taken off the enquiry under very strange circumstances. He subsequently left the police force to write a book about the affair. The following is an extract.

We were told by the RUC that contact with Republican elements in strongly Catholic areas around Lurgan and Armagh was just not possible. The risks to us of death or capture were unacceptable to the RUC, and they could not guarantee our safety without a massive show of strength from both police and Army. For very good operational reasons this type of heavy display, put on merely to enable us to speak to a possible witness in our enquiry, was quite out of the question. I knew, however, that to do the job properly I had to spend many hours with some elements who are hostile to the RUC, and to us as representatives of the British government. The problem posed was a serious one. The RUC was unequivocally opposed to our seeing these people, and the personal risk to us was chillingly real. If I insisted, then a big police/Army operation would reluctantly have to be arranged. We learned that the people we wished to see would not under any circumstances come near a police station. They would not come to us, and we were strongly advised not to go to them. We had reached an impasse, and I had to decide the best way round it.

I knew very well that the RUC's concerns for us were valid and sincere. But I decided that if my investigation was to mean anything it had to be seen to have tried consciously to overcome these difficulties. The method we subsequently adopted worked very well. A member of my team would make contact with a relative of one of the deceased, usually by telephone, or through a third party, and a firm appointment would be made for two of my officers to be at the local priest's house at a prearranged time. The RUC car would, at my request, drop us off a mile or so away and we would walk to the appointment. Often the young woman detective on my team made appointments direct by travelling alone to a house, usually on foot. I shall never know what the risks were, but I do know that if the IRA had wished to pick any of us off they could easily have done so. None of us was armed, at any time, while in Northern Ireland. I believe that our willingness to meet the families of the deceased on their own ground, unarmed and alone, quickly established with them our honesty of purpose and neutrality, and was probably the biggest single factor in our making the progress that we did. It has been said that in doing so I exposed myself and my team to unnecessary danger and that I risked creating a new crisis. I take a different view. I regarded our approach as having elements of necessary danger, but I saw no honest alternative. Contact with people who could help the enquiry was crucial. The members of the team knew what they were doing, but none of them expressed reservations or resentment. Even with the benefit of hindsight I would still conduct this aspect of the investigation in exactly the same way. A view could be taken that the IRA had nothing to gain by the assassination of me or of any member of my team. I was, after all, investigating obvious wrongdoing by their sworn enemies, the RUC, and until my investigation was completed I could not be accused of conducting a whitewash. I knew, however, that the fact of our walking alone and openly in certain housing estates in Lurgan and Armagh must have caused earnest discussion among terrorist elements. They knew I was there and they obviously decided I should be given a chance to complete the job.

One of the parish priests, Father Murray, was an enormous help in easing my entry into strongly Catholic enclaves in Armagh. He acted as a neutral intermediary, and lent his authority and experience to us. He was as sceptical as every other Catholic we met about what my enquiry would actually achieve, but his hopes for Northern Ireland persuaded him to keep on trying. The people we met were wary of us at first, one or two openly hostile, but all of them quickly settled into a type of polite but puzzled co-operativeness. After a while, as confidence in our objectivity grew, we were invited to some individual homes in order to take long written statements, often lasting for several hours. The television would be turned off, the kettle switched on, and this curious vignette of a British policeman sitting on their settee, taking details of the killing of their relatives and friends by other policemen, was studied at close hand. Occasionally the semi-formality of it all would be broken and someone would ask whether we were playing an elaborate game with them. None of them believed the investigation would actually achieve anything or lead to prosecutions of policemen, and several of the people I saw said prophetically that I would never finish the enquiry, particularly if it began to threaten the RUC or the British government. I recall one community leader saying to me that he just could not understand why we all seemed to be taking the whole business so seriously. He advised me to 'get in and get out' as quickly as I could: 'Tell them [the government] what they want to hear – that the RUC are a fine brave force. Whatever you say will make no difference over here – the lid has to be kept on. Only the RUC can do it – you won't be allowed to lift it off.'

I especially remember one young man in a house in Lurgan asking to see my Manchester warrant card. He gazed at it and said, 'I can't believe I have a Brit. cop in my house. I'm glad I've got witnesses because my kids will never believe it when they grow up.' Many of the older people we saw were like the people of inner-city Manchester, the area in which I was born and brought up. They gave us a respectful and polite welcome into their homes and I saw the same ornaments, wallpaper and furniture that I have seen so many times in similar houses in Manchester. But above all, they were interested in the reasons for our being in their homes. They were world-weary people, seemingly resigned to a never-changing situation but with a resilience and spirit which left its mark on my team and on me. I never had an opportunity to thank them for their hospitality, or indeed to thank the priests and others who helped us. Perhaps belatedly I can do so here – for their cool detachment and their careful choice of words, for an acceptance of our honest desire to do a professional job, but especially just for their presence and influence in those early edgy days.

Many members of the RUC, some at senior level, never accepted our need to meet and speak with Republican families. Their view, expressed forcefully and often, was that my regarding them as important witnesses, with something to contribute to my enquiry, gave Republican groups a spurious and undeserved respectability. My team was told that the IRA would regard our interest in those families as a publicity coup, and would exploit my presence on the estates for everything it was worth, either by ridiculing what they would describe as the attempts of the British government to cover up a cover-up, or by resurrecting the emotions surrounding the deaths of two years earlier. I was seen as offering myself to the IRA as a ready-made and willing stick with which they might beat the security forces. I was very well aware then that my decision to regard relatives of the dead men, and other Republican families, as potentially legitimate witnesses was seen as naive and harmful by RUC Special Branch. Such is their understandable antipathy, hatred even, towards the IRA, they are absolutely convinced that any official contact, no matter how remote, can only add to the political stature of terrorists. I do not agree with them. The Special Branch and my team never saw eye to eye about this. I had given careful thought to it, and had recognized the propaganda value to IRA publicists, but nevertheless decided I was morally and professionally bound to do as I did. I have had plenty of time to reflect on the way I dealt with this part of my investigation, and I still believe I was right.

A strange sort of detached respect for us seemed to grow. No doubt what we represented – the police and the British Crown – was detested. We, as individuals, however, were tolerated, obviously on occasion against instinctive judgements. We were the first and possibly only policemen many of those people will ever meet in a non-confrontational, almost friendly, atmosphere.

The spokesmen for the families of the dead men were usually solicitors. They were wary towards us, very conscious, it seemed to me, of the contempt I would be held in by some policemen for entering their clients' homes. It was fascinating to see at close quarters the relationship between police and some defence solicitors in Northern Ireland. It was quite unlike anything I have ever experienced in England. In this country a defence solicitor – even the most anti-police or devious of them – is treated by policemen as a professional. He may be spoken to very coolly, in a carefully guarded way, but he will be acknowledged as doing a job. I saw very little of that type of relationship during the long days I spent at Crumlin Road Crown Court, particularly where the cases which interested me were concerned. For me and my team the Courthouse was a convenient place where we could speak to solicitors, tell them of our intentions and retain their co-operation. It was a place for new introductions, for appointment-making and courtesy contacts with a number of solicitors who specialize in representing Republican families.

The atmosphere in the big hall was electric whenever we spoke to any of these solicitors. We felt open resentment and distrust from many of the RUC officers gathered in small groups around us. I recall one conversation with a youngish RUC uniformed sergeant who left his group and approached me angrily as I walked away after a very short conversation with a solicitor representing Martin McCauley, the youth who survived the shooting at the Hayshed. The sergeant came up to me and said, 'May I speak to you, Mr Stalker? Do you know who that was you were speaking to?' I replied, 'Yes – it was Martin McCauley and his solicitor.' The sergeant said, 'The solicitor is an IRA man – any man who represents IRA men is worse than an IRA man. His brother is an IRA man also and I have to say that I believe a senior policeman of your rank should not be seen speaking to the likes of either of them. My colleagues have asked me to tell you that you have embarrassed all of us in doing that. I will be reporting this conversation and what you have done to my superiors.'

I was surprised at his studied vehemence, although I recognized his comment for the honest bigotry it clearly was, and I let the matter go. But what he had starkly illustrated to me was the bitter depths of hatred even among professionals. I began to understand just why my presence in Northern Ireland was resented so much. I had again lent respectability to alleged terrorists – a solicitor and client – merely by talking to them. This conversation with the sergeant also showed me how easy it would be in the Province to have one's name included in Special Branch files and minds as having 'possible Republican sympathies'. An open conversation in a public place with a solicitor who performs his duty to the courts was, it seems, probably sufficient evidence of such 'sympathies'.

From *Stalker* by John Stalker, London: Harrap Ltd. 1988, pp. 44–49. © John Stalker Ltd.

cop (sl.) policeman – 3 *RUC, SAS, IRA* →**G** – 6 **subsequently** later, afterwards – 9 *Republican* →**G** – 10 *Lurgan* [ˈlɜː(r)gən], *Armagh* [ɑː(r)ˈmɑː] towns south of Belfast – 16 *display* here: show of strength – 17 **witness** s. o. who has seen s. th. happen – 20 **hostile** unfriendly, opposed to – 22 **to pose (a problem)** to ask or present a question or problem – 23 *unequivocally* clearly, without doubt – 25 *chillingly* frighteningly – 32 *impasse* dead end, obstacle that prevents progress – 35 **valid** legitimate, correct – 36 **investigation** enquiry – 41 **the deceased** the dead – 42 *third party* a neutral person – 67 **crucial** [ˈkruːʃəl] of the greatest importance – 69 **reservations** doubts – 70 **hindsight** wisdom after s. th. has happened – 74 **assassination** killing (of a public figure) – 78 *whitewash* (fig.) cover-up – 86 **parish priest** the priest in charge of a church and its community – 89 *intermediary* person who negotiates between two sides – 95 **wary** cautious, not trusting – 103 *vignette* symbolic little picture – 104 *settee* [–ˈ–] sofa – 109 **elaborate** [ɪˈlæbərɪt] complicated – 111 **prosecution** the taking of legal action against – 128 *warrant card* identification of a police officer – 140 **weary** tired – 142 *resilience* ability to recover and survive – 147 *detachment* emotional distance – 151 *edgy* nervous – 158 *spurious* false – 161 **coup** [kuː] great success – **to exploit** to make (incorrect) use of – 165 *to resurrect* to bring to life again, to revive – 174 *Special Branch* anti-terrorist/anti-subversive branch of the police – 175 *antipathy* [–ˈ–––] strong dislike – 178 *stature* reputation, public standing – 191 **to detest** to hate – 198 **solicitor** lawyer – 207 *devious* tricky – 220 *courtesy contacts* contacts to establish good relations – 233 *the Hayshed* on 24 Nov. 1982 the two boys were shot (one fatally) after entering a hayshed where guns had been hidden – 244 **to embarrass** to put in an awkward position – 247 **vehemence** strongly expressed feeling – 249 **bigotry** [ˈ–––] intolerance and prejudice – 255 *alleged terrorist* s. o. who is believed to be a terrorist – 259 *files* official lists and documents – 264 **evidence** s. th. which tends to prove s. th.

1. *What was John Stalker's task, and how did he set about doing it?*
2. *What did the RUC object to? For what reason or reasons?*
3. *Why did he reject the RUC's advice?*
4. *How did the witnesses and families of the deceased react to Stalker's visits?*
5. *What impression do you get from this extract about relations between the police and the Catholic (Republican) community?*
6. *Stalker tells us that he was regarded by many in Northern Ireland as "naive" (l. 173). Do you think he was?*
7. *In February 1989 the solicitor referred to in lines 227–233 was assassinated. Does what you have just read help you to understand why someone should want to kill him?*

7 The Sound of Marching Feet

All efforts to conciliate the Catholics of Northern Ireland have met with strong resistance from a certain section of the Protestant community. In 1974, for example, the new Belfast "power-sharing" Assembly was brought down by a general strike. A more recent development to meet with their disapproval has been the Anglo-Irish Agreement of 1985. Such Protestant fundamentalists are represented by Rev. Ian Paisley's Democratic Unionist Party (DUP).

Ivan Foster is Democratic Unionist Party member of the Northern Ireland Assembly for Fermanagh. In the Anglo-Irish agreement, as in the moral depravity all around him, he sees the signs of the apocalypse and hears the sound of marching feet. [...]

Reverend Ian Paisley

Ivan Foster sees the breakdown of law and order in the Northern state as linked to moral depravity. "I would be very concerned for the future of any country that continues to liberalise and liberalise and liberalise. Because it is an indisputable fact that alongside recent developments, liberal trends, there has been an increasing social problem regarding law and order, in the home, in the marriage, in the schoolroom or just on the streets.

"It may be argued that there is no link, but I think there is a link. I recognise as a Protestant that if a Protestant loses his Protestantism, then he loses all motivation for opposing a United Ireland. It's immaterial to him who serves the Guinness as long as it's served. Under what flag doesn't matter, the political consequences of change don't matter. I see the danger of a population undermined by libertine trends that is gradually abolishing its spritual heritage, its spritual base, and since its spiritual base was always the source of its opposition to a United Ireland philosophy, that opposition will disappear. [...]

Jim Wells is young, smooth, a Queen's graduate from the rich farming land of South Down, which he represents for the DUP in the Assembly. [...]

Where Jim Wells stands is with the planter stock he came from. He believes in a separate Protestant race in Northern Ireland and in preserving the purity of that race. […]

"It's a fact, not something to be debated about. We don't feel British, we *are* British. This is what Southern people cannot grasp.

"They believe that because we live on the island of Ireland that we regard ourselves as Irish. Nothing could be further from the truth. I think we regard ourselves as more British than the British. I think we're the first to stand for the National Anthem and to show respect for the Queen, even more so than many mainland British subjects, many of whom have intermarried with Pakistanis and West Indians and allowed a dilution of their Britishness. That hasn't happened here and we remain militant British subjects. Here there's been very little intermarriage with immigrants or with native Irish. And mixed marriage is frowned upon; I only know of one mixed marriage in my experience. We at least have maintained our Britishness, even if other parts of Britain have wavered somewhat."

Jim Wells is one of those who does the frowning on mixed marriage. "I am totally opposed to mixed marriage. Of course I am. First of all because of the authoritarian attitude of the Roman Catholic church, which demands that the children must be brought up as Catholics, but secondly because I believe that anyone who indulges in a mixed marriage is betraying the Protestant cause. There's no excuse for mixed marriages in the North, not like in the south where the small number of Protestants means that to be blunt there's many a young man and young girl who wouldn't marry at all if they didn't marry a Roman Catholic. There's no problem such as that in the North where there are plenty of suitable Protestant partners. I would be against anything that would lead to a dilution of the Protestant population of this province." […]

That deep-seated evangelical Protestantism is central to the DUP, and the fear of religious persecution is a large part of their fear of a United Ireland. Jim Wells sums up the objections to Catholicism: "We find much of Roman Catholic doctrine repugnant. I find repugnant the fact that any man has the right to forgive sins, that Christ can be recreated on the altar of the Mass Sunday after Sunday; that the Virgin Mary is regarded as a deity that can be prayed to, who can forgive sins and heal the sick and all that, that shrines which can supposedly move in Ballinspittle or wherever it is can delude thousands into believing that there are some magical powers. That is superstition of almost African tribal levels, which we find totally repugnant, and we just do not wish a situation to arise where we would find ourselves dominated by that type of system. If the priests can get twelve million pounds for an airport in the middle of a bog in Mayo, what can they not do to Protestants? Many Protestants would just have to get up and leave under those circumstances, they just wouldn't tolerate it.

1 **to conciliate** to overcome the distrust and hostility of – 2 *power-sharing Assembly* see Chronology – 4 *Anglo-Irish Agreement* see Chapter IV (pp. 54–55) for details – 5 *Rev. Ian Paisley* Free Presbyterian Church leader, since the 1950s most prominent spokesman of the extremist Protestants – *DUP* →**G** – 7 *Northern Ireland Assembly* →**H**, 1982–86 – 9 **depravity** [dɪˈprævɪtɪ] badness, evil – 17 **indisputable** undoubted – 26 *immaterial* unimportant – 27 *Guinness* [ˈgɪnəs] a dark beer brewed in Dublin – 30 *libertine* extremely liberal, permissive – 32 **heritage** what is passed down from previous generations – 36 *Queen's* Queen's University, Belfast – **graduate** s. o. who has a university degree – 38 *Down* county south-east of Belfast – 40 *planter stock* the race of people who were "planted" in Ulster in the 17th century (→**H**) – 46 **to grasp** to understand – 56 *dilution* a watering-down of some quality – 61 **to frown upon** to disapprove of – 64 *to waver* to behave uncertainly – 73 *to betray a cause* to let down what one should believe in – 76 *to be blunt* frankly, to be honest – 85 *deep-seated* deeply rooted – 87 **persecution** cruel treatment of a group of people – 90 **repugnant** [rɪˈpʌgnənt] very unpleasant – 94 **deity** god – 97 *Ballinspittle* a village in Co. Cork with a shrine where in 1985 several people claimed to have seen the statue of the Virgin Mary move – 98 **to delude** to deceive – 100 **superstition** belief in magic – 105 *airport... in Mayo* a reference to the airport opened in 1986 at Knock, Co. Mayo, a place of Catholic pilgrimage (to the surprise of the many opponents of the project, it has proved an economic success) – **bog** marshy land

"My view of the south is coloured by the experience of my relatives who refused to live in the south. My wife's mother was born in the Irish republic and all her folk lived in Cavan and Monaghan. And one hears the experiences that they went through as Protestants in the Irish republic, and the way that they were discriminated against overtly and covertly, and the way in which for instance they found it difficult to be educated except by nuns and priests and found it difficult to get teaching jobs because they couldn't speak Irish. Their civil liberties, in the form of birth control, divorce, that sort of thing, were controlled by a Catholic-dominated state, and many thousands of them were forced to come up here and live in Northern Ireland. When we see the way they were treated in the south, then that is enough to convince us that we don't want to go there. But could I say that even if the streets of Dublin were paved with gold and even if Ian Paisley were allowed to write the constitution, and if Dublin was a state flowing with milk and honey and motorways – which you don't have by the way – and all the paraphernalia of a western civilised society, we still wouldn't be interested." [...]

Gregory Campbell, in another world might have been a socialist. The Waterside in Derry where he has always lived is no bastion of Loyalist privilege. "My parents weren't members of any political party, and paid no heed or interest to politics. My father was a serviceman in the navy. We were just the average Protestant family in Northern Ireland. The thing that pushed me into involvement in politics was the whole Civil Rights scenario, and the whole nationalist complaint and agitation that they were getting a raw deal. That was the clincher for me because I saw on the television screens and read in the papers where people like John Hume and the beginnings of the SDLP were agitating for Catholic rights, and at the same time I saw the type of community that John Hume was from and the type of living standards that they had, which were very similar to my own. [...]

"I joined the Young Unionist Movement and I found myself campaigning for people that I was still socially opposed to. I found myself campaigning for people like Robin Chichester-Clarke, brother of the former Prime Minister, and to me that person was on a different social scale, a different planet, to me. The guy was a highbrow Tory who cared very little if at all for working-class Protestant people, who were the people who were electing him. And gradually I moved over to the Protestant Unionist Party, which at that time, 1970–1971, was just changing over to the DUP." [...]

The DUP is implacably opposed to any role whatsoever for the Irish government in the running of Northern Ireland. Even if that role is minor, "consultative" and cosmetic, they see it as the beginning of the end, the road to Armageddon. "While we're interested in the fine print of an agreement, and we will study it carefully, the fact that for the first time the Dublin government are going to be given an input in any way, that will be enough to trigger off all of our opposition, whatever the fine print," says Gregory Campbell. "If Tom King were to say to us, 'Look, we're only consulting Dublin about the colour of the lamp-posts,' that is sufficient for us to say that for the first time Dublin has a toe in the door. It's only a few months or a few years from advising us on the colour of the lamp-posts, to telling us what way we will conduct the traffic, to what way we will dress the police, to what way we will arm them. If Dublin is to have a say in any respect, if they are to have a say in that the

113 *Cavan* [ˈkævn], *Monaghan* [ˈmɒnəhən] Ulster counties in the Republic – 117 **overtly** [əʊˈvɜːtlɪ] openly – **covertly** [ˈkʌvətlɪ] secretly – 130 **to pave** to cover the ground – 134 *paraphernalia* [ˌ–––ˈ––] all the things belonging to s. th. – 140 *loyalist* →**G** – 141 *to pay heed* to pay attention – 143 **navy** marine forces – 148 *to get a raw deal* (coll.) to be treated unfairly – 149 *clincher* (coll.) s. th. which "clinches" (i. e. decides) s. th. – 151 *John Hume* Civil Rights leader, later leader of the SDLP (→**G**) – 164 *guy* (sl.) man – *highbrow* on a high social or intellectual level – *Tory* Conservative (→**G**) – 171 *implacably* uncompromisingly – 174 **minor** very small – 176 *Armageddon* the Last Judgement – 180 *input* chance to contribute s. th. – **to trigger** to set off, to spark off – 182 *Tom King* British Secretary of State for Northern Ireland at the time

Flags and Emblems Act is to be repealed, because Peter Barry and Garret FitzGerald have said it is offensive to nationalists and must be repealed, something that is regarded as small beer, then the British government will be sitting down and listening to the views of the Dublin government. Sovereignty is sovereignty. You either are sovereign over a part of a country or you are not. You either have absolute control or you do not. If Dublin has a consultative role, that is the beginning of the end. I would see the final day had arrived whereby Ulster had finally been sold, and we would have no other option but to exhaust the constitutional process and then proceed as quickly as possible to arming ourselves and to fighting. [...]

One man [who would fight] is Ivan Foster. As a minister, his theology does not prevent him from wielding a gun. "Modernism has equated Christianity with pacifism, which is a load of rubbish. It is useful to throw in here that title which is given to the Lord in the Bible where it says of him that he is a man of war. These Anglo-Irish talks are entering a phase where it is very possible that the state will become a tyrant and say to me as a British citizen that I am going to lose a part of my citizenship because a foreign state is going to be given a role in the running of a part of the United Kingdom. It is a Presbyterian doctrine, ground out in the hard mill of the days of persecution in Scotland, that when the government, or the king as it then was, forsakes his lawful role and begins to enforce his will on the people contrary to the contract that exists between him and the people, then the king is no longer the lawful head of state, he has become a tyrant. And it is a Christian's duty to resist a tyrant.

"I would have no hesitation. I wouldn't be joining the army of Ulster as a chaplain. I would be joining it as Joe Bloggs, an ordinary foot soldier. I would not be infringing my conscience or the word of God, but acting in complete obedience to both. I would have no compunction, not in the least. I know how to use a gun."

From the article "Fire and Brimstone" by Fintan O'Toole in *Magill* (Dublin), November 14, 1985, pp. 16–27.

193 *Flags and Emblems Act* a law forbidding the display of Republican symbols in N. I. – **to repeal** to take back or undo (a law) – 194 *Peter Barry* Minister for External Affairs in the Republic of Ireland at the time – *Garret Fitzgerald* Taoiseach [ˈti:ʃɒk] (Prime Minister) of the Republic of Ireland, leader of the Fine Gael party (→**G**) at the time – 195 *nationalist* →**G** – 197 *small beer* s. th. unimportant – 199 **sovereignty** the right of a country to decide its own affairs without outside interference – 206 **to exhaust** here: to use up, to finish using – 212 **to wield** [i:] to hold and use – **to equate** to say, s. th. is equal to s. th. else – 223 *Presbyterian* →**G** – 226 **to forsake** to give up, to abandon – 231 **to resist** to fight against – 234 *chaplain* [ˈtʃæplɪn] army priest or minister – 236 **to infringe** to go against – 238 *compunction* doubts, scruples

1. *What are we told about the social background of Ivan Foster, Jim Wells and Gregory Campbell?*
2. *What have they got in common?*
3. *What are Jim Wells' views on Catholicism, mixed marriages, and national identity?*
4. *Why did Gregory Campbell* not *become a socialist? What political conflicts did he come up against in the Unionist Party?*
5. *What support does Ivan Foster find in the Bible for his views?*

IV Focus on the Republic

1 A New Day for Ireland

There's a heartbreaking beauty in the Irish landscape: dark cliffs against the sea, fingers of green land pushing out against the sea, meadows of yellow gorse and slate blue rock, brown boglands, sometimes a house and two figures in the distance. More often the landscapes are empty, and so we can populate them with our dreams, the ideal of man, uncorrupted, living in harmony and touch with the earth and the sea.

At times it seems that Dublin too, founded in the 9th century by Vikings and given its present appearance in the 18th and 19th centuries, has escaped the 20th, as if the century, like the clouds, has merely passed over, leaving a soft, magical city. [...]

And so, amid our own complications, a vision of Ireland has often restored us: one place, a small island on the edge of Europe, where time has stood still.

But Ireland is changing. Pursuing a policy of rapid industrialization, the Republic of Ireland (in Gaelic, Éire) experienced in the past decade unparalleled growth and prosperity: Industrial output doubled, incomes soared; farmers found that their gains rose 140 percent in five years.

With prosperity came other changes. More Irishmen were coming back to the island than were leaving it. More were marrying and at an earlier age. Ireland now boasts not only the fastest growing population in Western Europe but also the youngest, half under 25 years of age.

Membership in the European Economic Community has given it new diplomatic and trade links with the Continent, lessening its centuries-old dependence on Britain. Such gains have brought new confidence. [...]

So Ireland joins the 20th century: To that lovely landscape, long marked by ruined Norman keeps and medieval monasteries, we must now add factories and suburbs.

From the article by John J. Putman in *National Geographic*, Washington D.C., April 1981, pp. 442, 446.

4 *gorse* a bush with prickly leaves and yellow flowers – **slate** a grey-blue stone used as roof tiles – 5 *bogland* marshy land – 7 **to populate** *here:* to fill with s. th. – 9 *uncorrupted* pure, not spoiled – 23 *Éire* [ˈeɪrə] – 24 *unparalleled* unlike anything before – 25 **to soar** to rise sharply – 31 **to boast** to have and be proud of – 42 *keep* fortified tower – **medieval** [ˌmedɪˈivl] of the middle ages – **monastery** [ˈmɒnəstrɪ] building where monks live together

1. *What impression is given here of the character of the Irish Republic?*
2. *What changes have happened in the last few decades?*
3. *This picture of children waiting for a school bus in a remote part of Ireland was used in an advert encouraging foreign investment. Discuss its message.*

The Irish Economy

For most citizens of the Irish Republic, the conflict in the North seems very far away. More immediate are the economic problems which have beset the country since independence. Here, in a simplified form, are the main phases in the country's economic development.

The 1920s: Cut off from its industrial North, and with few natural resources, the Free State's economy was overwhelmingly based on agriculture, and the standard of living was correspondingly low. Emigration was the traditional solution for the many who could not make a decent living from the land. One big success of this period was the beginning of the rural electrification scheme, based on hydro-electric power.

1930s–50s: Efforts to develop native industries were hampered by an "economic war" with Britain, and then by the country's isolation during World War II. The farmers also suffered economically. Emigration reached a new peak in the 1950s. In spite of a high birth-rate, the population was declining.

1960s–70s: A period of economic recovery and rapid industrialization. As well as promoting native industry, the state began to encourage foreign investment by offering tax exemptions and other favourable conditions. EEC membership proved especially beneficial to Irish farmers. Tourism was recognized as a major industry. Living standards rose rapidly, and by the mid-70s the population was rising again.

The 1980s: After a promising start, economic problems grew. Many young people, including those trained for the country's newly developed computer industry, were again forced to emigrate – to Britain, to the USA, and (a new development) to EC countries.

2 What Sort of Country is This?

Bob Geldof, a young Dubliner who was to become a successful rock singer and the organizer of Live Aid, here tells of his efforts in the early 70s to start a business in Dublin. While working in Canada he had picked up what seemed to be a promising idea: a small ad magazine that is free for advertisers.

Things had begun well enough. Brian Devon and his wife had come back from Vancouver with us and had put up £2,000 for the new paper. That doubled my own initial capital from my Canadian savings. I had commissioned a survey from magazine distributors who were enthusiastic and said that it was the most positive report they had produced for any new paper in the previous five years. I had a deal with a printer in Bray which gave me thirty days' credit, enabling me to publish four weekly issues before I had to pay for the first one. I had persuaded three of the participants in a leading car rally which was covered live on television, to paint their vehicles in *Buy & Sell* colours. I had some pretty girls, all old friends, wearing sashes advertising the publication, canvass the response of housewives outside supermarkets with dummy issues. Armed with all this research and promotion and accompanied by the heavyweight solicitor and accountant I had engaged, I went to the bank.

I didn't open my mouth but let the professionals set out the case. The two Dublin evening papers were full of classified ads at that time. The demand for personal advertising and sales would continue to flourish. Even with a downturn in the economy there would be steady growth, as in a recession the demand for cheap second-hand goods and therefore such advertising would continue. The magazine would be distributed free in certain problematic areas and would therefore circulate outside metropolitan Dublin which would gain it national advertising as opposed to the restrictive city-only advertising which was the bane of so many publications. The several contingency plans were outlined and the accountant explained that it was on conservative estimates that he projected that I would have repaid all loans within six months and would be in a healthy profit by the end of the year.

The bank manager listened in silence. Then he sat back in his chair. He put his fingers together in a gesture of such pomposity that I knew he was going to say something ludicrous.

'Mr Geldof, how old are you?' I told him I was twenty-four. 'Then I suggest that you come back to us when you are forty and have something to show for yourself.'

I lost my temper and raged about the difference between Ireland and North America and told him that the country was in a mess precisely because of people like him. Yes, I was only twenty-four but here I was offering to take eleven people off the dole and give them jobs as typists and telephonists and here he was saying that all twelve of us should continue to live off the state rather than use our initiative to create wealth. I raged at him, doubtless in his mind proving his point about my relative youth and immaturity, but by then it was clear that there was no way I was going to get the money from him.

At this point I still had approaches to make to other banks, credit unions and finance houses but, even more pressing if the paper was to work, I had to organize the telephone lines for the new business. Devon's father-in-law had given us the use of a building near where I had worked in the meat factory. We moved into the front room and set up shop. Despite the bank's refusal to help I decided to push ahead. We needed at least six phone lines, all preferably coming in to one number. I rang the phone company.

'Forget it,' they said.

'I can't forget it, this is my job. How long will it take?'

'It'll take at least three years and then you could probably only have two.'

I couldn't believe it. In Canada if you wanted a new phone you had a choice of companies and you got it that day. 'But that's ridiculous,' I said.

'It's too bad, you mean, we're up to our neck in work. We can't meet the demand, especially in the Ballsbridge area.'

I knew it was impossible talking to this man or any other but I still could not accept the situation. I phoned the government and got the number for Conor Cruise O'Brien, then the Minister for Posts and Telegraphs. To my surprise I was given an appointment to meet him. Conor Cruise O'Brien is a journalist, editor, diplomat and intellectual. He listened to my argument, my 'What Sort of Country is This?' schtick.

At the end he said, 'I know, I agree, but I can't do anything.'

'But you're the Minister,' I said.

'I know, but I can't dig the holes and put down the lines. The whole thing's a bloody mess.' He was very honest.

From *Is That It?* by Bob Geldof, London: Sidgwick and Jackson; reprinted from the Penguin edition, pp. 123–125.

9 **to commission** to order and pay for a service – 10 **survey** a study of a particular situation – **distributors** those whose job it is to send goods to the shops – 14 **deal** business agreement – *Bray* seaside town south of Dublin – 16 **issue** example of a magazine – 21 *sash* piece of cloth worn round the waist or over one shoulder – 22 *to canvass* ['––] to approach people individually in a systematic way for a political or commercial purpose – 23 *dummy* not genuine – 25 *heavyweight* here fig.: impressive – **solicitor** lawyer who advises clients but does not normally appear in a criminal court – 26 **accountant** financial advisor – 30 **classified ads** small advertisements classified under different headings – 38 **to circulate** to reach the public – 39 **metropolitan** of the city area – 42 *bane* s. th. that causes problems – *contingency plans* [–'tındʒ––] plans

for different situations that might develop – 50 **pomposity** [–ˌpɒs––] false show of dignity – 51 **ludicrous** ['–––] ridiculous – 57 **to rage** to express great anger – 62 **dole** (sl.) unemployment benefit – 68 **immaturity** state of being too young and undeveloped – 73 *pressing* urgent – 94 *Ballsbridge* expensive residential area in south Dublin where most embassies are located – 104 *schtick* (sl.) line of talk

1. *How did Bob Geldof plan to promote his magazine?*
2. *Why did he think it had a good chance of success?*
3. *What unexpected problems did he run into?*
4. *What is the "difference beteween Ireland and North America" (ll. 57–58) that Bob refers to? Can you explain it?*

3 The Fugitive

Violence had preceded the formation of a new Irish state, and it was followed by more violence: a year-long Civil War between those who accepted the Treaty with Britain, and those who rejected it as an unacceptable compromise.

After their defeat, most anti-Treaty Republicans gradually came to terms with the new state. Many participated in its government. But even after the Free State was unilaterally declared a Republic in 1937, there were some who held on to the old dream of a united Irish Republic, and saw violence as the only way of achieving it.

Here, travel writer Dervla Murphy describes her childhood encounter with such an individual.

The year 1944 was marked by some strange experiences. […]

One harsh, dark March afternoon a squealing hinge made me look through the kitchen window. A young man was entering the cobbled yard from the abandoned cinema, which meant that he had climbed our eight-foot garden wall. Yet I felt not at all alarmed, possibly because I was never prone to be made uneasy by the unconventional. Or it may simply have been because the young man looked so amiable and vulnerable. As he stood at the back door I noticed that he seemed rather apprehensive and very tired. He was tall, broad-shouldered and handsome, and I marked a Kerry brogue when he gave his name as Pat Carney and asked, diffidently, if he might see one or both of my parents.

In the living-room my mother's bath chair was close to the sulky wartime fire of wet turf. She seemed oddly unsurprised by our visitor's original approach route and my curiosity was further sharpened when she asked me to leave her alone with Pat. Ten minutes later Pat was back in the kitchen. He said that he had been invited to stay for a few days and that my mother would like to speak to me. Then, pausing inside the living-room door, I did begin to feel alarmed. Never before had I seen my mother looking so distraught. Mrs Mansfield and San Toy were coming to tea so there was no time to waste on euphemisms. In a couple of sentences I had been told that Pat was on the run, wanted for the murder of a Dublin detective-sergeant. He had come to us as a protégé of my father's elder sister who, never

fugitive ['fjuːdʒɪtɪv] a person fleeing from s. th., usually the law – 11 **to squeal** to make a piercing, high-pitched sound – 12 **hinge** metal part on which a door or gate swings – 13 *cobbled* paved with smooth, round stones – 14 **abandoned** given up, left unused – 17 **to be prone to** to have a tendency to (do s. th.) – **uneasy** worried or uncomfortable – 20 **amiable** ['eɪmɪəbl] friendly – **vulnerable** easily hurt – 22 **apprehensive** worried and fearful – 23 **handsome** good-looking – 24 *to mark* to notice – *Kerry* county in southwest Ireland – *brogue* strong Irish accent – 25 **diffident** lacking confidence – 27 *bath chair* wheeled chair for a disabled person (named after the English town of Bath) – 28 **sulky** ill-humoured; here: slow-burning – 38 *distraught* upset and confused – 39 *San Toy* Mrs Mansfield's dog – 40 **euphemism** pleasant expression for s. th. bad – 41 *on the run* (coll.) fleeing from the law – 44 *protégé* [ˌprɒtə'ʒeɪ] (French) s. o. who is helped by a more influential person having recognised the validity of the post-Treaty Irish government, was an active member of the illegal IRA. On no account must any caller be allowed to see our guest or any trace of his presence. As I continued to stand by the door, paralysed with astonishment, my mother made a gallant preliminary bid to sort out the ethics of the situation. "This young man is a criminal though he regards himself as a patriot. No doubt his elders are chiefly to blame. They are using his muddled, foolish idealism. But we can talk about it later. Now please show him his room and give him a meal."

I walked down the hall in a joyous daze. This was the stuff of which fantasies are made, yet now it had become part of the reality of my own life. I was to prepare a meal for a man on the run who would be hanged if caught. My mother might have saved her breath. Of course Pat was not a criminal, or muddled or foolish. He was a most glorious patriot, heroically dedicated to the reunification of Ireland. No one had ever suggested that my grandfather and father were criminals because they belonged to the Old IRA. One had to be logical. I was badly jolted when I discovered how strongly my father disapproved of Pat. But then I reflected that he (my father) was very old (forty-three). And I made allowances for the fact that at that age some people just can't have the right reactions any more.

Listening to my parents, I gathered that for some days they had been half-expecting Pat without knowing exactly why he was on the run. Now they were disagreeing vigorously about how they should deal with him and it gave me a certain sardonic satisfaction to observe them both being inconsistent; at twelve, one likes the feet of clay to appear occasionally. My father should have been the one to welcome – or at least tolerate – Pat, while my mother (given her ancestry) should have been the one to reject him. Instead, my father coldly argued that it would be sinful to shelter someone who had deliberately killed an innocent man in the course of a seditious campaign against a lawfully established government. And my mother warmly argued that it was unthinkable, sinful or no, to betray someone whose coming to our home was an act of faith in our humanity. She insisted that allowances must be made for Pat's sick idealism. To which my father, sprung from generations of rebels, replied austerely that it would prove impossible to govern the state if hectic emotionalism were to be accepted as an excuse for murder. My mother then suggested that he should go at once to the gardai barracks and report on Pat's whereabouts. But he didn't.

My parents seem never to have debated the ethics of capital punishment; presumably they accepted it, in theory, as the appropriate penalty for murder. Yet had it not been employed in Ireland during the Forties, as part of the government's anti-IRA campaign, they might well have refused to succour Pat. When such a decision can lead directly to a death sentence it requires more moral courage, or moral arrogance, than either of my parents possessed.

From their point of view an awkward situation was being compounded by the need to impress on me that giving refuge to Pat did not mean condoning his crime. In the end they gave up pretending to unravel this tangled skein for my benefit, which was sensible of

45 **validity** legitimacy – 46 *Treaty* →**H**, 1921 – 47 *IRA* →**G** – 48 **trace** sign – 51 *gallant* brave – *preliminary bid* first attempt – 54 **elders** parents and older relatives – 55 **muddled** confused – 59 **daze** state of dizzy confusion – 67 **to dedicate** to give wholly to some purpose – **reunification** uniting again – 73 **to reflect** to think, to consider – 80 **vigorously** strongly – 82 *sardonic* mocking, bitter – 83 **inconsistant** illogical, holding contradictory beliefs – 84 *feet of clay* (fig.) weakness – 87 *given*... assuming; with s. th. as a know fact – **ancestry** ['–––] family history – 91 *seditious* conspiring to cause disturbance or rebellion – 94 **to betray** to hand over a friend to an enemy – 99 *austere* [–'–] here: strict, pedantic – 103 *gardai* [gɑːr'diː] (Gael.: Gárdaí Siochána = Guardians of the Peace) police force of the Irish Republic – 107 **capital punishment** the death penalty – 108 **appropriate** suitable – 112 *to succour* to help and protect – 118 *to compound* to make more complicated – 120 **to condone** to approve of – 121 *to unravel* [–'rævl] ... *skein* [skeɪn] to straighten out a ball of thread that has become tangled (here fig.)

them since I well knew that they were incapable of unravelling it for their own. I had in any case already come to my own conclusions and was only listening to their dutiful dissertations out of politeness. Yet I vaguely sympathised with their discomfiture; though they repudiated Pat as a violent man their consciences compelled them to allow for the fact that he saw himself as a soldier fighting a just war – a dilemma that in present-day Northern Ireland has again become familiar to many.

Pat stayed with us for a fortnight, but he and I never referred directly to his peculiar status and he made no attempt to influence me politically. We played round after round of rummy and he gave me lessons in map-reading and taught me how to whistle through my fingers so piercingly that I can be heard two miles away. To me this marvellous companion seemed a magic sort of person, an intelligent grown-up who had retained all the wondering enthusiasms of childhood. And my intuition was right. It was Pat's tragedy that he had never outgrown either the innocence or the ruthlessness of youth.

My parents also became very fond of Pat and deeply concerned about him. Night after night they argued patiently in futile attempts to make him see the error of his ways. Soon he seemed a member of the family – quite an achievement, in view of the strains imposed on all the adults concerned by his presence in the house. Had he been detected under our roof, my father would not have perjured himself by denying any knowledge of his identity and so would certainly have been imprisoned – as his sister was soon to be, on Pat's account.

Our guest was careful never to go too near a window and any knock at the door sent him rushing upstairs. Remembering how I relished all this melodrama, I wonder now if I fully understood that we were truly dicing with death. But my light-hearted approach may well have helped by easing the tension generated between the three adults. Pat knew that I took the game seriously enough to keep all the rules, and I was made deliriously proud by his entrusting to me the addressing and posting of his letters. One morning I went into his room to leave fresh linen on the bed and saw an automatic by the pillow. For years this was to rank as the most thrilling moment in my life. I tingled all over at the romance of that weapon – symbol of Adventure! – gleaming black and lethal on the white sheet. It never occurred to me that in certain circumstances it could be used to kill the local gardai, the fathers of my playmates. But then it was impossible to associate the gentle, considerate Pat with any form of violence or cruelty.

One evening Pat said good-bye instead of good-night and when we got up next morning he was gone. We heard nothing of him for several months, but his luck did not hold. He was eventually captured in my aunt's house, while asleep, and tried in Dublin before the Military Tribunal. Then he was hanged by the neck until he died, at eight o'clock in the morning on December 1, 1944. His real name was Charles Kerins.

From *Wheels Within Wheels* by Dervla Murphy, London: John Murray Ltd. 1979; reprinted from the Penguin edition, pp. 118–121.

126 *dutiful* done only because it is one's duty – 128 *discomfiture* feeling of being uneasy or uncomfortable – 129 **to repudiate** to reject – 138 *rummy* a card game – 147 **ruthlessness** cruelty and lack of scruples – 150 **futile** useless, ineffective – 155 **to detect** to find – 156 **to perjure o. s.** to lie under oath in a court of law – 163 **to relish** [relɪʃ] to enjoy greatly – *to dice with* to play with, to risk – 167 **to ease (tension)** to lessen, to soften – 170 *deliriously* madly, extremely – 174 *automatic* kind of pistol – 175 **to rank** to have a certain position – 176 **to tingle** to shiver with excitement – 178 **lethal** [ˈliːθl] deadly – 181 **playmates** friends that s. o. plays with

1. *Summarize the incident described here.*
2. *How did Dervla Murphy feel about helping to hide a fugitive from the law?*
3. *Discuss her parents' attitudes. How "logical" (l. 70) were they?*
4. *How would you behave in such a "dilemma"?*

Constitutional Controversies

No one person has had more influence in shaping the present-day Republic of Ireland than Eamon De Valera. A veteran of the 1916 Easter Rising, the War of Independence, and the Civil War, he founded a new party, Fianna Fáil, which came to power in the late twenties.

While suppressing illegal IRA activities just as his predecessors in government had done, De Valera's policy was to change the nature of the state from within. His new Constitution, which was adopted by referendum in 1937, made the country a Republic and broke the remaining ties with Britain and the Commonwealth – though this was not officially recognized by Britain until 1949.

This 1937 Constitution is still in force today. In spite of its many admirable qualities, a number of its articles have caused considerable controversy. Consider the following:

Article 2. (Territory) *The national territory consists of the whole island of Ireland, its islands and the territorial seas.*	Still in force. Article 2 is seen by many as encouraging violence to overcome partition. Others call on it to condemn any cooperation with the N. I. state. (See text IV 5.)
Article 8. (Language) *1. The Irish language as the national language is the first official language.* *2. The English language is recognized as a second official language.*	Now quite uncontroversial, at the time this article was resented by some members of the Anglo-Irish (Protestant) community who did not identify with Gaelic culture.
Article 41. (Family Rights) *3.2. No law shall be enacted providing for the grant of a dissolution of marriage.*	Still in force. The referendum to remove the ban on divorce failed in 1986 (see text IV 4).
Article 44. (Freedom of Religion) *3. The state recognizes the special position of the Roman Catholic Church as the religion professed by the great majority of its citizens.*	Removed by referendum in 1972, leaving the uncontroversial, non-sectarian parts of the article.

Critics of the Catholic-influenced aspects of De Valera's Constitution were appalled when in 1982, as a result of a referendum, Article 40 (Personal Rights) was amended to include a ban on abortion.

4 A Vote for Forever and Ever

Efforts to make the Republic a more pluralist society received a serious setback in 1986, when the divorce amendment was rejected. The following Time *article sums up the situation.*

IRELAND

A Vote for Forever and Ever

Referendum on divorce delivers a resounding no

For more than a month, throughout the Republic of Ireland, newspapers were occupied, minds preoccupied, with the bitterly divisive issue. Hand-lettered signs dotted street corners with a single simple message: VOTE NO. In Dublin's Parnell Square, demonstrators waved placards that mockingly read, DOES DIVORCE WORK? ASK LIZ TAYLOR. Not far away, several women trapped in unhappy marriages chained themselves to the railings of parliament. Bishops decried the proposal from pulpits, while the country's most influential paper, the *Irish Times*, defended it. Everywhere the debate raged on: Should Ireland permit divorce?

The final answer last week was a thundering no when 1.4 million of the republic's 3.5 million citizens went to the polls to vote on a constitutional amendment that would have changed the 49-year-old prohibition against divorce. The proposal was defeated by a thumping 63% to 36%. In rural areas the amendment was put down by as much as 8 to 1.

The outcome dealt a humiliating blow to the already wobbly ruling coalition headed by Prime Minister Garret FitzGerald, who had personally led the campaign in favor of divorce. It also sealed the country's own marriage to the Roman Catholic Church and set back hopes of a closer alliance with Northern Ireland, the republic's predominantly Protestant neighbor. Said Pro-Divorce Activist Margaret Geaney, choking back tears: "The majority has spoken and said, 'We don't give a damn about you.' "

Throughout the campaign, supporters of the amendment stressed humanitarian issues, pointing to the suffering of an estimated 70,000 Irish couples saddled with untenable marriages. Under present law, husband and wife must either endure their life together, however unpleasant, or unofficially separate. The latter course brings further problems: since children born of other unions will be illegitimate, inheritances will go not to them but to the legal spouse, however long separated. The amendment would have permitted couples to divorce after they showed that their marriage had failed for five years and that there was no hope for its rescue.

Defenders of the wedding bond played upon the fears of countryfolk, especially women, stranded in economically ravaged areas, where unemployment is often well over 50%. One study cited by Alice Glenn, a breakaway member of parliament from FitzGerald's Fine Gael party, revealed that 93% of divorced women with children in the U.S. live below the poverty line. "A woman voting for divorce," Glenn often repeated, "is like a turkey voting for Christmas."

Opponents of the amendment also scored heavily by stressing that divorced spouses could lose their property as well as inheritance rights to their land. That struck a raw nerve in a country that is still 40% agricultural. "If there's one thing an Irish farmer loves more than his wife," said an Irish farmer, "it's his farm."

For its part, the Catholic Church officially remained relatively low-keyed during the referendum campaign. But when the going got tough, so did some of the clergy. "God says no to divorce," pronounced Bishop Jeremiah Newman of Limerick.

The defeat of the amendment means that the Irish Republic is one of only a handful of countries in the world where divorce is still illegal. Malta and the Philippines are others. The setback weakens FitzGerald's chances of re-election in 1987. Though the opposition Fianna Fáil party remained neutral on the referendum, it made clear its opposition to the amendment. The Prime Minister's failure to legalize divorce could thus hasten his departure from power.

Article in *Time*, New York, July 7, 1986, p. 33.

Anti-divorce campaigner Alice Glenn speaking in Limerick.

4 **divisive** likely to divide people – 5 *to dot* here: to be seen everywhere – 7 **placard** [ˈplækɑːd] poster on a stiff background – 9 *Liz Taylor* Elizabeth Taylor, much-married (and divorced) film star – 12 *to decry* to speak against – 13 **pulpit** [ˈpʊlpit] place from which a priest speaks in church – 20 *the polls* an election or referendum – **amendment** change made (in a constitution) – 23 *thumping* (coll.) overwhelming – 27 **wobbly** shaky, in danger of losing power – 42 *saddled with* forced to keep s. th. one doesn't want – 43 **untenable** [–ˈten––] impossible to uphold – 44 **to endure** to put up with – 49 **inheritance** [–ˈher––] what is passed on from one generation to the next – 50 **spouse** [spaʊz] husband or wife – 55 **bond** tie – 58 **ravaged** [ˈrævɪdʒd] devastated – 61 *Fine Gael* [ˌfiːnə ˈgeəl] →**G** – 71 *to strike a raw nerve* to touch a sensitive point – 76 *low-keyed* restrained – 77 **referendum** a national vote on a particular proposal – 78 *when the going got tough* (coll.) when the campaign got more hard-hitting – **clergy** priests and bishops – 85 **setback** [ˈ––] sudden reverse (in s. o.'s progress) – 87 *Fianna Fáil* [ˌfɪənə ˈfɔːɪl] →**G**

1. *What were the arguments for retaining the constitutional ban on divorce?*
2. *What attitude did the Catholic bishops take?*
3. *How will the result of the referendum be seen in Northern Ireland?*

5 The Anglo-Irish Agreement

The following is from a Fine Gael party leaflet issued in 1985 after the signing by Garret Fitzgerald and Margaret Thatcher of an important Agreement between their two Governments.

How does this Agreement improve the position of Nationalists?

First of all in the preamble to the Agreement the British Government, amongst other things, recognises the need to acknowledge the rights of the two major traditions that exist in Ireland, both the Unionist tradition and the tradition of "those who aspire to a sovereign united Ireland achieved by peaceful means and through agreement".

They also commit themselves to a "society in Northern Ireland free from discrimination and intolerance, with the opportunity for both communities to participate fully in the structures and processes of government". Moreover, *if a majority of the people of Northern Ireland give their consent to Irish unity the British Government commit themselves to "introduce and support" in the Westminster parliament, legislation to give effect to this.*

Secondly, the British Government agrees to the establishment of an Intergovernmental Conference concerned with Northern Ireland and with relations between the two parts of the island, in order to deal on a regular basis with "all fields – political, security, legal, economic, social and cultural – which come within its competence."

Does this Agreement not involve accepting partition – in fact, copper-fastening it? Does it not undermine the constitutional position?

No. It does none of these things. Of course it accepts the inescapable fact that Ireland is not at present united and faces the question of what can be done to help Northern Nationalists in this situation without detriment to the Unionist tradition.

But is the Conference not to be consultative only – will it have any real power?

It is not merely consultative. It involves much more than a mere obligation on the British Government to ask the Irish Government for its views on certain matters. It imposes a legal obligation on the two governments to make "determined efforts through the conference to resolve any differences... in the interests of promoting peace and stability".

How will the Conference actually operate?

It will involve regular and frequent meetings of Ministers of the Irish Government with British Ministers in Belfast, and special meetings can be called at any time at the request of either side. These regular and frequent meetings of the Inter-Governmental Conference of Ministers will be serviced by a joint secretariat which will be established by the two Governments in Belfast and will operate on a continuing basis between Ministerial meetings.

What about the RUC?

At its first meeting the conference will consider ways of underlining the policy that the RUC and the armed forces in Northern Ireland discharge their duties even-handedly and with equal respect for the Unionists' and the Nationalists' identities and traditions.

What effect is the Agreement likely to have in Northern Ireland?

Of course it is impossible to predict what will happen in an area where there has been so much violence and where the two communities are so polarised. But it is our hope that the effect on the nationalist minority of the extensive involvement of the Irish Government in the processes of government in Northern Ireland, will have a major impact on their sense of alienation from the structures of government, the security forces and the judicial system in Northern Ireland.

Doesn't the Agreement carry risks however?

Yes – of course it does. Any Agreement to take action in Northern Ireland is bound to stir up hostility at both extremes – amongst the IRA on one side, which owes its existence to the alienation of the minority community, and amongst extremists on the Unionist side also. As both Governments have made it clear on occasions before the signature of this Agreement it cannot exclude the possibility of greater unrest, and even violence, in the immediate aftermath of the signing of the Agreement. But the prospect of giving the minority in Northern Ireland for the first time in sixty-five years a fair deal, of eliminating their legitimate grievances, and of removing the ground from under the IRA, makes it worthwhile to take these risks, and, we believe, requires us to do so. Of course it is always easier to do nothing, in the hope of avoiding blame for anything that may go wrong, but such an attitude would be totally irresponsible in the face of the tragedy of Northern Ireland.

1 *Fine Gael* [ˌfiːnə ˈgeəl] →**G** – 4 *nationalist* →**G** – 5 *preamble* [prɪˈæmbl] introductory passage – 9 *unionist* →**G** – 13 **to commit o. s.** to make a promise that cannot be undone – 32 *partition* →**G** – *to copper-fasten* (fig.) to make secure and long-lasting – 39 *without detriment to* without harming – *RUC* →**G** – 66 *even-handedly* fairly – 71 **to predict** to say what will happen in the future – 78 **impact** [ˈ––] effect – 79 **alienation** feeling of not belonging, of being strangers – 80 *security forces* (in Northern Ireland) the British Army, the RUC and the UDR (→**G**) – *judicial system* the courts of law – 86 *IRA* →**G** – 96 *to give s. o. a fair deal* (coll.) to treat s. o. fairly – 97 **grievance** [ˈgriːvəns] complaint

1. *What is the Anglo-Irish Agreement supposed to achieve?*
2. *Judging by the questions posed, what are the main criticisms of the Agreement in the Republic?*
3. *What are the "risks" (l. 82)? (Consider also what you know of Northern Protestant reactions to the Agreement.)*

V The British Perspective

1 An Irish Problem – or a British Problem?

The following contributions were written nearly two hundred years apart, but both address the same question.

Edmund Burke, 1796:

Against all reason, experience, and observation, many persons in Ireland have taken it into their heads that the influence of the Government here has been the cause of the misdemeanour of persons in power in that country, and that they are suffering under the yoke of a British dominion. I must speak the truth – I must say that all the evils of Ireland originate within itself; that it is the boundless credit which is given to an Irish cabal that produces whatever mischiefs both countries may feel in their relation. England has hardly anything to do with Irish government. I heartily wish it were otherwise; but the body of the people of England, even the most active politicians, take little or no concern in the affairs of Ireland. They are, therefore, by the minister of this country, who fears upon that account no responsibility here, and who shuns all responsibility in Ireland, abandoned to the direction of those who are actually in possession of its internal government; this has been the case more eminently for these five or six last years; and it is a system, if it deserves that name, not likely to be altered.

I conceive that the last disturbances, and those the most important, and which have the deepest root, do not originate, nor have they their greatest strength, among the Catholics; but there is, and ever has been, a strong republican Protestant faction in Ireland, which has persecuted the Catholics as long as persecution would answer their purpose…

Edmund Burke

From a letter written by Edmund Burke to Thomas Keogh, Esq. in Beaconsfield, November 17, 1796; reprinted from the collection of Burke's writings *Irish Affairs*, ed. Matthew Arnold, new edition, London: The Cresset Library 1988, pp. 414–415.

Liam de Paor, 1971:

Both in the Republic of Ireland and in Great Britain, public opinion has swung to and fro during the years of trouble in Northern Ireland. Undoubtedly, to many people in Britain the whole business must seem wearisome and inexplicable. *The Spectator* and other conservative journals have referred to 'the Irish mess' in terms which suggest that the whole situation is due to some defect in the Irish character. This is to miss the point. It is a British mess. […]

I have laid the emphasis on the British connection, since it is British attempts to govern in Ireland through a colonial regime which seem to me to have given rise (not only in the case of Ulster) to most of the difficulties in what for long was known as 'the Irish question' (although an Irishman might well think that it were better called 'the British question'). British statesmen have not been prepared to devote to Ireland the amount of time and attention its good government required. They have attempted, in all Ireland in the more distant past and in Northern Ireland in the recent past, to rule Ireland through a colony. This has failed. 'Planters and natives' can undoubtedly come to an agreement in Ireland, perhaps an agreement to continue in some form the partition of the country, but it seems to me essential that those who are responsible for government in Ireland should be rooted in the country and committed to it – and ultimately dependent on Irish resources and initiatives to solve Ireland's problems. What keeps the sterile quarrel of Orange and Green alive is the constant presence of the third party, Great Britain.

From *Divided Ulster* by Liam de Paor, Harmondsworth: Penguin 1971, pp. XVI–XX.

(*Burke*) 4 **misdemeanour** [ˌmɪsdɪˈmiːnə] bad behaviour – 6 *yoke* a curved piece of wood joining two animals to a cart; here fig.: oppressive domination – 7 *dominion* rule – 9 **boundless** endless – *credit* here: freedom to act – 11 *mischiefs* harm, damage done – 14 *the body of* most of – 19 **to shun** to reject – 20 *to abandon to* to give up, to leave to the mercy of – 31 *republican* →**G**; here: against the monarchy
(*de Paor*) 5 **wearisome** tiresome – 16 *Ulster* →**G** – 26 *planter* here: settler (who is "planted" in a foreign country) – 29 *partition* →**G** – 32 **to be committed to** to be closely involved in – 35 *Orange and Green* (fig.) loyalist and republican (→**G**)

1. *There is one point on which both writers agree. What is it?*
2. *Who does Burke blame for the troubles in Ireland?*
3. *Where does Liam de Paor put most blame?*
4. *What was the political situation in Ireland when both pieces were written?*

Present British Party Programmes on Northern Ireland

The Conservative Party:	**The Labour Party:**
The constitutional status of N. I. is a matter for its people to decide. It must therefore remain part of the UK unless a majority in N. I. votes for changes.	Irish unification by consent is the long-term goal. No constitutional change will be made without the consent of the people of N. I., but this aim should be actively pursued; i. e. no Unionist "veto on political progress".
Direct Rule from Westminster can only be temporary. A devolved N. I. Government is desirable, but its form must be agreed on by the democratic parties in N. I.	Devolved N. I. government is preferable to Direct Rule, but only if it contains a power-sharing element acceptable to the minority.
The Anglo-Irish Agreement (1985) was signed in order to improve co-operation between the Irish Republic and the UK especially on matters of security, and to help the minority identify with N. I. institutions.	The Anglo-Irish Agreement needs to be implemented more actively. More co-operation with Dublin is necessary to achieve harmonization of the legal, educational and economic systems north and south of the border. EC Regional Funds should be used to further this aim.

(Party programmes, continued)

Conservative:
Strong measures against terrorism have been necessary: the Prevention of Terrorism Acts (1984 and 1989) give greater powers to the police; the Criminal Evidence Order makes it easier to convict a suspect who remains silent; non-jury Diplock courts (→**G**) are necessary in N. I. Suppporters of violence are to be disqualified from election to parliament or local government.

The Conservative Government is encouraging more private enterprise in N. I. in order to create more jobs. Discrimination in employment is being combatted. More integrated, non-denominational education is desirable, and financial assistance is available for such private schools.

Labour:
The Prevention of Terrorism Act is rejected as ineffective and unnecessary. Labour will restore a suspect's right to remain silent, end detention without charge, work towards restoration of jury trials for all offences, and take measures to increase public confidence in the RUC.

Privatization schemes are rejected as a form of economic withdrawal from N. I. Instead, steps must be taken to end poverty and extreme social inequality. Affirmative action will be needed to overcome sectarian discrimination in employment. Financial support will be available for integrated schools, and for Irish language teaching.

The Social and Liberal Democrats (SLD) share many of the Conservative policies, but demand "partnership in government" in N. I., and recognition of the "Irish dimension" through a British-Irish Parliamentary Council. Stronger police powers should be combined with an independent tribunal to deal with complaints. As a long-term goal they suggest a confederation of the UK and the Irish Republic.

2 Calling Their Bluff

Tony Benn represents the left wing of the Labour Party. Here are his personal views on Britain's involvement in Northern Ireland.

I'm now absolutely certain that the reason Britain is in Ireland has nothing to do with the reasons given to the public. Britain is there for military purposes. When no longer useful, Zimbabwe and Hong Kong were handed over. I think the Tories are prepared to hand over Gibraltar. In the end we'll probably hand over the Falklands. No one is ever going to convince me that there is some deep commitment in the Conservative Cabinet to the maintenance of the rights of the Protestants in the North. From the very beginning, and certainly after the First World War, it was the defence argument that was dominant.

When I read that during the Second World War, Churchill had offered De Valera Irish unity in exchange for their neutrality without bothering to tell Northern Ireland leaders, I began to think afresh. [...]

I think that it's useful for everybody to examine the background of their own thinking. It gives you a certain depth and strength, and means that you don't get diverted by arguments that are suddenly thrown in in some current controversy about a particular act of violence which is almost inevitable in the present situation.

The loyalist veto is a very clever technique. Keeping the loyalists on a string means that sectarian divisions can always be whipped up.

At the same time, knowing that there is a loyalist majority, the government can shield behind it, claiming that its policies represent the majority. The veto would have been brushed aside by Churchill's war-time offer. If the Republic decided to join NATO, I think it would be brushed aside again today.

The loyalist veto is basically the technique by which the British military maintain their presence in the North. It deepens divisions because it is one of those skillful and cunning techniques that fulfills its own prophecies. As long as there is a loyalist veto, no loyalist extremist has to bother about the basic civil rights of the minority. They know that if they go on ignoring the rights of that minority, no matter how strong the reaction against them is, they can always rely upon the army or the SAS to come in and protect the status quo. It stimulates violence rather than promotes any co-operation.

The veto is the trigger that brings in the troops; it brings in detention without trial, strip searches, the PTA, H-blocks, Diplock Courts and supergrass trials.

That veto has no constitutional validity whatsoever, and it restricts the rights of the British Parliament as much as it does the Irish. Supposing we had a vote in the House of Commons in favour of British withdrawal from Ireland. The fictional veto would mean we could not activate that policy, that it would be subject to a veto by a majority of a minority in Ireland. The exposure of this wholly undemocratic concept is essential. […]

If it were clear to the Protestants and the Catholics in the North, to the people of the Republic and the people of Britain that there was to be a date after which there would be a termination of British jurisdiction, then I think this would release into the debate a whole range of arguments that are now held back. For one thing, the whole 'security' argument would assume quite a different aspect; it would release a great deal of money at present being spent on the 'emergency' into potential projects that are not now available. In this context, the trade unions would be bound to feel they could begin to play a new role. A lot of the tension would go out of the situation. I'm also sure that after a declaration of this kind, the military activities and energies of the nationalist movement might well be directed into more constructive purposes.

I personally find it very hard to accept the argument that you can't act for fear of a bloodbath triggered off by the loyalists. If we lived in a fair world, this threat of violence to prevent a political settlement would earn the same denunciations as the nationalist violence has. But where would the loyalists have to go? They would be living in an Ireland in which they were required to play some part, not in one from which they were excluded. I think that calling the 'Carson bluff' or however you might describe it is an absolutely integral part of any successful negotiations.

From Tony Benn's contribution to *Ireland After Britain*, ed. Martin Collins, London: Pluto Press 1985, pp. 131–134.

to call s.o.'s bluff to challenge s.o., and thus show that they are bluffing – 8 *Tories* Conservatives (→**G**) – 11 **commitment** strong involvement – 16 **dominant** most important – 18 *(Sir Winston) Churchill* British Prime Minister during World War II – *(Eamon) De Valera* Irish Prime Minister at various times from the 30s to the 50s; later President of the Republic (see also Info Box p. 52) – 19 *neutrality* →**G** – 21 **afresh** anew, again – 25 **to divert** to send off in a different direction – 28 **inevitable** unavoidable – 30 *loyalist* →**G** – 31 *to keep s. o. on a string* to keep control of s. o. – 32 **sectarian** based on religious divisions – 34 *to shield* here: to hide (behind a shield) – 43 **cunning** very clever – 44 **prophecy** prediction, statement about the future – 47 *minority* in N. I., the Catholic community – 51 *SAS* →**G** – 54 *trigger* (fig.) s. th. which starts a process – 55 **detention** here: imprisonment, internment – 56 *strip search* thorough search of prisoners who are forced to take off their clothes – *PTA* the Prevention of Terrorism Act (see Info Box p. 58) – *H-Blocks* H-shaped buildings of the Maze Prison, near Belfast (→**G**) – *Diplock Courts* trials without a jury (→**G**) – 57 *supergrass* police informer, member of a terrorist group who gives evidence against a one-time comrade – 72 **termination** end – *jurisdiction* rule – 82 **tension** feeling of worry in the face of danger – 92 **denunciation** condemnation – 97 *Carson* see Info Box p. 16 and →**H**, 1912
(*Cartoon p. 60:*) *to waive a rule* to say a rule does not need to be kept

1. *Tony Benn rejects "the reasons given to the public" for maintaining British power in Northern Ireland. What are they? (Some are mentioned here, others you may know from other texts.)*
2. *What, in Benn's opinion, is the real reason? How does he support his argument?*
3. *What is the "loyalist veto" (l. 30)? Discuss how democratic or undemocratic it is.*
4. *According to Tony Benn, what course of action should Britain take?*
5. *What are the potential dangers of this course of action? What does Benn think of them?*
6. *In lines 55–57, a number of very controversial security measures are mentioned. Look them up in the Glossary and Info Boxes. Discuss why they were introduced.*

Britannia waives the rules

The picture and the caption are both parodies. Can you explain what is being parodied?

3 We Will Never Surrender to the IRA

Here is part of Prime Minister Margaret Thatcher's speech to the Conservative Party Conference at Brighton in October 1988.

It was the first time the Conference was held in Brighton since 1984, when an IRA bomb blasted the Grand Hotel where many leading politicians were staying. Five people were killed, and Mrs Thatcher herself narrowly escaped injury.

Conservatives need no sermons from Socialists on the rule of law. [...] Year after year, they will not support the Prevention of Terrorism Act – an act which is vital to the defeat of the IRA and which has saved so very many lives. I find that very hard to forgive.

In this country and in other democracies, the enemies of civilisation and freedom have turned to the gun and the bomb to destroy those they can't persuade. The terrorist threat to freedom is world-wide. It can never be met by appeasement. Give in to the terrorist and you breed more terrorism. At home and abroad our message is the same. We will not bargain, nor compromise, nor bend the knee to terrorists.

In our United Kingdom, the main terrorist threat has come from the IRA. Their minds twisted by hatred and fanaticism, they have tried to bomb and murder their way to their objective of tearing more than a million citizens out of the United Kingdom. The truth is that the whole IRA campaign is based on crushing democracy and smashing anyone who doesn't agree with them.

To all those who have suffered so much at their hands – to the Northern Ireland policemen, prison officers and their families, to the soldiers, the judges, the civil servants and their families – we offer our deepest admiration and thanks for defending democracy and our thanks for facing danger while keeping within the rule of law – unlike the terrorist who skulks in the shadows and shoots to kill.

We thank too the security forces who had the guts to go to Gibraltar to give evidence to the inquest, demonstrating conclusively that they acted at all times within the law and to save lives – the lives of countless people who would have been killed had the IRA fulfilled their murderous purpose. What a pity it is that there are still some in this country not prepared to accept the verdict of the jury, so great is their prejudice against the security forces. What comfort that must be to the terrorists.

We will work to increase co-operation in security between the sovereign governments in London and Dublin. We will work to involve both Protestants and Catholics fully and fairly in the economic and political life of Northern Ireland. But we will never give up the search for more effective ways of defeating the IRA.

If the IRA think they can weary us or frighten us, they have made a terrible miscalculation. People sometimes say that it's wrong to use the word never in politics. I disagree. Some things are of such fundamental importance that no other word is appropriate. So I say again today that this Government will *never* surrender to the IRA. *Never.*

Reprinted from *Margaret Thatcher: Speeches to the Conservative Party Conference 1975–1988,* London: Conservative Political Centre 1989, pp. 139–140.

8 *Prevention of Terrorism Act* see Info Box p. 58 – 10 *IRA* →**G** – 17 **appeasement** giving in to terrorists or aggressors in the hope of achieving peace – 39 *to skulk* to hide, waiting for a chance to strike – 42 *the guts* (coll.) the courage – *Gibraltar* →**H**, 1988 – 43 **inquest** court inquiry into the cause of death – 49 **verdict** conclusion

1. *What is Margaret Thatcher's view of terrorism? What does she see as the consequence of appeasement?*
2. *For whom does she express particular sympathy?*
3. *For discussion: How important is it for those "defending democracy" to keep "within the rule of law" (ll. 36–38, 44)?*
4. *Discuss the remark attributed to Margaret Thatcher in the cartoon below. How does it link up with the views expressed in her speech?*

"The only solution to the Irish problem is to understand that no solution works."

Glossary

The following is a list of terms commonly used in connection with Northern Ireland and Anglo-Irish relations. It includes the most important political groups, movements and parties, major religions, and a selection of the historical, political and cultural concepts relevant to the topic.

Anglican Church: A union of Churches which includes the Church of England and the Church of Ireland. The latter is the largest of the →Protestant Churches in Ireland as a whole, but in N. I. its members are outnumbered by the →Presbyterians. Anglicans in Ireland are mainly of →Anglo-Irish descent.

Anglo-Irish: 1. A term referring to any connections between Britain (or England) and Ireland. 2. Irish people (North and South) who are descended from English settlers of the 13th–17th centuries. They are culturally distinct from both the native Irish and the →Ulster Scots, who arrived later.

Alliance Party [əˈlaɪəns]: A moderate →unionist party in Northern Ireland. It was founded in 1970 and won support from conservative Catholics and Protestants, but has since declined in importance.

"B" Specials: A special armed part-time constabulary founded in 1920 to protect the new Northern Ireland state from subversives. Since it was recruited mainly from →Orangemen, many of them members of the →UVF, their activities added to the sectarian violence. Their abolition was one of the demands of the →Civil Rights Movement, and in 1970 they were replaced by the →UDR.

British: The term can be geographical (referring to the island of Britain) or cultural/political/historic. The people of N. I. are British citizens, and most (mainly the →Protestants) identify with Britain culturally.

British Isles: A totally unpolitical geographical term for the group of islands.

Catholic Church: About three-quarters of the population of Ireland as a whole are Roman Catholics (93% in the Republic, 30–40% in N. I. – no exact figures available). Although most members of the →Republican Movement have been Catholics, they have never had the official support of the Church, and many of its leaders have been excommunicated.

Celtic: The term is used to distinguish the native Irish population (mainly of Celtic origin, though with a strong Norman element) from the settlers of British origin. However, this distinction is not useful in N. I., since the →Ulster Scots are also of Celtic origin.

Civil Rights Movement: A movement to end discrimination against Catholics in N. I. which developed in the late 1960s.

Conservative Party: This British political party is not represented in N. I., but they have close connections with the →Unionist Party. In the 19th to early 20th century, British and Irish Conservatives (Tories) strongly opposed →Home Rule in the Westminster Parliament.

Diplock Courts: Since 1973, alleged terrorists in N. I. have come before special non-jury courts, to avoid the danger of intimidation by the IRA or other organizations. These courts are named after Lord Diplock, whose 1972 Report recommended their introduction. Another innovation was to allow convictions on the basis of "supergrass" evidence, i. e. of police informers or former terrorists.

DUP (Democratic Unionist Party): In 1971, the more radical members of the N. I. →Unionist Party broke away and formed a separate party. Their leader is Rev. Ian Paisley. The DUP still cooperates closely with what is now called the Official Unionist Party (OUP).

Éire: The Gaelic name for Ireland. Its use (common in Britain and among N. I. Protestants) to refer to the →Republic of Ireland is based on a misunderstanding. The 1937 Constitution gives it as the (Irish Gaelic) name of the state, because this constitution claims the whole island as its territory.

Fenians [ˈfiːnjənz]: Irish →nationalist secret society founded in 1858 with the aim of overthrowing British rule in Ireland. The name derives from "fianna", the legendary band of warriors led by Finn Mc Cumhaill [ˈfɪn məˈkʊel]. The movement failed, but gave rise to a series of other organizations with similar aims: the Irish Republican Brotherhood (IRB), the Irish Volunteers, the socialist Irish Citizen Army, and later the →IRA. "Fenian" is sometimes used today in N. I. as a derogatory term for →republicans or even Catholics.

Fianna Fáil [ˌfɪənə ˈfɔːɪl]: One of the two large (and equally conservative) political parties in the Republic of Ireland. The Gaelic name means "soldiers of destiny". It developed from the radical →republican, anti-Treaty side in the Civil War that was fought 1922–23. The party rejects violence, but upholds strong republican traditions, and the idea of →neutrality.

Fine Gael [ˌfiːnə ˈgeəl]: One of the two large (and equally conservative) political parties in the Republic. The Gaelic name means "family of the Gael". It developed from the pro-Treaty side in the Civil War of 1922–23. Today it is more inclined to support the status quo and to cooperate with Britain; on social issues it tends to be more liberal than its main rival →Fianna Fáil.

Gaelic: The term refers to the language and culture of the native Irish (Celtic) people, but also of the Highland Scots. The Lowland Scots who settled in Ulster (→Ulster Scots) do not, as a rule, identify with Gaelic culture, nor do the →Anglo-Irish – except for those who make a conscious effort to assimilate.

GAA (Gaelic Athletics Association): A sports organization which encourages and organizes what they call "Gaelic games", especially hurling and football. With the Gaelic League, which promoted the language revival, it played an important part in the national revival in the late 19th century. It is still very strong in the Republic and among the Catholic community in N. I. Gaelic games are organized on an all-Ireland basis.

H-Blocks: A complex of H-shaped buildings in the Maze prison, near Belfast. They were built in 1976 to house prisoners convicted of terrorist offences, who no longer enjoyed the "special category" status of political prisoners. For →republicans, the term came to symbolize the ill-treatment of prisoners; the "H-Block Campaign" focussed on this issue.

Home Rule Movement: The 19th century parliamentary movement to re-establish the Irish Parliament (which had been abolished in 1800) without leaving the →United Kingdom. It was supported by the British Liberal Party and the Irish Parliamentary Party.

Irish: Like →"British", this term can be geographical (of the island of Ireland) or cultural/political/historical. The →Protestants of N. I. differ as to whether it applies to them. The word can also refer to the original Celtic language of the country, to distinguish it from the closely related Scottish Gaelic.

Irish Free State: Previous name (1920–37) for what is now the →Republic of Ireland. Before the Republic was declared, it had been a member of the Commonwealth.

INLA (Irish National Liberation Army): A terrorist group which broke away from the →Official IRA in 1975. They combine left-wing ideas with acts of extreme violence.

IRA (Irish Republican Army): A paramilitary organization founded in 1919 to overthrow British rule in Ireland. It remained active after 1921 with the aim of achieving complete independence for all of Ireland. However, it had declined to unimportance over the years. It was given a new lease of life in the early 70s, after the collapse of the →Civil Rights Movement, and especially after the arrival of the British Army. It soon split into two wings (both illegal): the →Official IRA and the →Provisional IRA.

Labour Party: There is a strong Labour Party in Britain and a small one in the Republic of Ireland, but neither is represented in Northern Ireland, where sectarian divisions have prevented the development of a united working class. (→SDLP)

Loyalist: A person who is loyal to the British Crown, and therefore a supporter of the Union with Britain. The term is almost interchangeable with →unionist. The vast majority of N. I. loyalists/unionists are →Protestants.

Nationalist: In Ireland, a person who supports the idea of an independent Irish nation; almost interchangeable with →republican.

Nationalist Party: For many years (1920s–60s) the only opposition to the ruling →Unionist Party in Northern Ireland. Since the →Civil Rights Movement it has been superseded by the →SDLP and →Sinn Féin.

Neutrality: Because of the dispute with Britain over Northern Ireland, the Republic remained neutral in World War II, and it has since developed a positive policy of neutrality in international affairs. The Irish Republic is therefore at time of publication the only non-NATO state in the European Community.

Northern Ireland: The official (though geographically inaccurate) term for the part of Ireland which remained part of the →United Kingdom in 1921.

NICRA (Northern Ireland Civil Rights Association): The coordinating body of the →Civil Rights Movement. It was founded in 1967, and included Catholics, Protestants, and a wide spectrum of political opinion among its membership.

Official IRA: This marxist wing of the →IRA was involved in the violence which broke out in the wake of the →Civil Rights Movement, but it has since declared a ceasefire.

Orange Order, Orangemen: An organization of →Ulster Protestants founded in 1795 with the aim of preserving Protestant rule and privileges in Ireland. It was named after their hero, King William of Orange. Up to the present, it has been successful in uniting Protestants of all classes against what they see as a common enemy.

OUP: →Unionist Party, →DUP

Partition: The division of Ireland into two parts with two separate parliaments by the 1920 Goverment of Ireland Act. It became effective in 1922.

Peace People: A N. I. movement which started in 1976 among people, mainly women, who were tired of the senseless slaughter. It cut across religious divisions and gained widespread support. Its leaders, Betty Williams and Mairead Corrigan, were awarded the Nobel Peace Prize for 1976. The movement has since declined to insignificance.

People's Democracy: A left-wing students organization active in the →Civil Rights Movement. Their best-known leader was Bernadette Devlin, who was elected to the Westminster Parliament in 1969.

Presbyterian Church: A →Protestant domination strongly influenced by the teachings of Calvin, very strong in Scotland (= Church of Scotland) and Northern Ireland, where it was brought by 17th century settlers.

Protestants: The Protestants of Ireland include →Anglicans, →Presbyterians, and Methodists. They make up about 5% of the population of the Republic, and over 60% of the N. I. population.

Provisional IRA (Provos): The more militant wing of the →IRA, which has remained an active terrorist organization in spite of the →Officials' 1972 ceasefire.

Republic of Ireland: Also Irish Republic. What was previously the →Irish Free State was declared a republic in 1937, though this was not recognized by Britain until 1949. Its constitution makes a territorial claim on the whole of Ireland, but recognizes that at the moment its laws can only apply to the 26 counties which left the →United Kingdom in 1921.

Republican: In Ireland, a person who supports the idea of a united Irish Republic independent of Britain. Though the movement was originally (18th c.) led by liberal→ Protestants, today most republicans are →Catholics.

RUC (Royal Ulster Constabulary): The police force of Northern Ireland, established 1922. It has always been an armed force (unlike that of mainland Britain) with anti-terrorist functions. Despite efforts to recruit from the Catholic community, it has remained a largely Protestant force.

SAS (Special Air Services). A unit of the British Army specially trained for under-cover activities. The SAS was founded during World War II, has been used all over the British Empire, and since 1969 in Northern Ireland.

SDLP (Social Democratic and Labour Party): A political party founded in N. I. in 1970 to further the aims of the →Civil Rights Movement, but also aiming at the eventual reunification of Ireland by consent. Today it usually gets the support of about two-thirds of the Catholic/Republican Community, most of the rest going to →Sinn Féin.